WALLOON WRITERS REVIEW

Seventh Edition

An annual collection of poetry, short stories, creative writing and nature photography inspired by Northern Michigan and the Upper Peninsula.

MISSION POINT PRESS

Walloon Writers Review
PO Box 2393 Petoskey, Michigan 49770
www.walloonwriters.com

Seventh Edition Editor: Glen Young
Founding Editor: Jennifer Huder
Cover Photography: Cascade ©Karen Walker

Seventh Edition, 2022
Walloon Writers Review (ISSN:

ISBN: 978-1-954786-94-3
Library of Congress Control Number: 2022906889

CONTENTS

Photography

INTRODUCTION

There are as many ways to lose yourself in Northern Michigan or the Upper Peninsula as there are ways to get lost. There are also many reasons, as time and space in the woods or near the waters can be restorative.

Sometimes the best way to lose yourself however, is through story. Whether poetry, prose, or photography, story can take us from where we are, whether sweeping us along in the current of a spring fast river, or dropping us into the canopy of an unmapped forest.

Story gives us something we didn't know we needed, and it gives us back what we yearn for most. We hope you will find all of this in the pages of *Walloon Writers Review, Seventh Edition.*

And what we find in getting lost in story is power in the form of something new; or time in the form of pause; or respite in the form calm.

There are stories here, in shapes and shades, that take us back to places we know, as well as those that urge us to spots that we might not recognize. Either way, the power or the pause or the calm illustrate what a vibrant place Northern Michigan and the Upper Peninsula are if we only look; they remind us how we are all fortunate to know this place, whether we live here or we visit.

As in earlier editions, there are new voices, familiar voices, and voices we have admired elsewhere, now a part of the *Walloon Writers Review.* In each case, whether poetry, prose, or photography, whether familiar or new, we are pleased to include the many ways these artists approach getting lost or losing yourself in the current or the grace of this remarkable region.

We hope you appreciate losing yourself, or getting lost, in the pages of *Walloon Writers Review, Seventh Edition.*

Glen Young

Adler Creek Trail *©Elizabeth J. Bates*

Soaring

Joyce Brinkman

In robin-blue sky
Upper Peninsula air
Lifts me with eagles

Becoming Lake Michigan

Joyce Brinkman

A family of four
birthed from the same
cold mother of ice, who
would carve your character,
then leave you hollowed
and low. Together you
welcomed life's warmed elixir,
matching the cerulean sky
in a day's dose of sunlight.
Feeding your euphotic zones
until explosions of watery creatures
claimed you for their home.

North Of The 45th

Edd Tury

I'd rather shiver than sweat
walk between the pines
rather than the bricks
breathe forest musk
not city funk

safer here
closer to the pole than the equator
less likely
to slide down the face of the earth
not likely
to wish I were somewhere else

Lake Treasure

Katy Klimczuk

Combing among the speckled rocks
And shells
Aqua
Mint
And seafoam green

Emerge

Edges soft and smooth
Once hidden below the depths
Lashing
Thrashing

Rise

Surface

Bringing unexpected delight
And beauty

Softened by water
Wind
Weather

Time

Much like us

Northern Light

Deda Kavanagh

sunrise
across the spider's
bridge-line

my steps
skirting the sky
in Lake of the Clouds

the loft of light
on grass flying off
the 9-iron

a thousand
silver starlings—noon light
on Walloon Lake

breaststroke
the widow's
sole solace

kites flying
over downtown Petoskey
telling tales

Sunshine Panacea

Lauren Driscoll

The sun has become my cure all
I soak in it for depression
And lather it on when I need love
I have found that sometimes I am the whole storm and others I am
only the raindrop
Some days I want to melt into the harbor and others I want to burn
into the sun
On days that she hides her glorious face,
I too cocoon into my shell, shiver in the shallow waters of the
state park and impatiently wait for
the clouds to part
At 2pm when the sky is robin egg blue and my tears have dried
I drag my flesh from the deserted dunes to the piles of
petoskey-pocketed pebbles
Peek through the rocks for treasures
Watch the seagulls disappear past evergreen waves and aged brick buildings
And say my devotions to Mother Michigan
I sing with the waves until it cures my depression
Just for the day, or maybe the hour
And count the minutes until she rises again

Autumn Palette ©*Jennifer Uehlein Reynolds*

Exposure

Jim Daniels

straits of mackinac

at   the beach
 eroding into dark

wind off Lake Michigan
fresh with   the wistful

what if   what
 if if if   end-

less with more
or less   desire

last mis-
 sives ex-
change
   of pulses

you know some-
body gonna
   gotta build

a fire breath
   inadequate
       against it

but still
you will warm

whatever skin
you still bare.

Wildcat Canyon Image

Christine Saari

I

Rich varied greens:
tamarack and balsam fir,
black spruce and white pine,
yellow grasses, thick moss,
blue sky, puffy clouds.
Wild wetlands along
A forest road.

II

A painter sits
in a blueberry patch
amidst this verdant scene.
A pad on her knees,
she aims to capture
what she sees:
Shades of green,
a touch of fall color,
the texture of rocks.
Not easy to paint
such rich complexity.

III

The photographer views
the lush landscape from afar.
For her the painter in the center
defines the image,
an image of man in nature.
The person is not dominant,
but the artist's presence
changes the feel of the place.
Hidden behind bushes and scrubs,
the photographer feels
like a deer.

IV

I view the photograph,
hanging on a gallery wall.
I see the image of an artist,
an artist painting a wetland
a wetland in a remote place.
Separated by time and space,
by three levels of experience,
I am there, nonetheless,
in the midst of this jewel
at Wildcat Canyon.

Sunrise Day 1369 Edgar Speer Mackinac Island ©*Melissa Seitz*

Littoral Zone

Jim Daniels

Peace of Superior
          ruined by a shout:
Nice, it's nice out here, huh?

Your wallet bloats with disappointment
in your sagging back pocket,
even in the lull of open water—
                    or shrinks?

Still wind, the impossible calm
          of an unnamed cliff.
Even grief takes a hike
in the calm of this water

and sand the color
          of that girl's hair,
the one who died.

We meet each other at last,
          you whisper to your reflection—
old joke, new laugh.

Moist

Jim Daniels

I know some people hate that word—
what can you say to those fans of *dry*?

Smell of humid August night in the woods
beside a secluded pond in Northern Michigan

that demanded we remove our clothes.
You know that we did, easing in

beneath the tiny bugs on the surface
to find each other below. You know

we had to surface for air and suffer
a few bites. It was worth it to find

the dark moist center of the earth.
If you've gotten this far, you know.

Monarch Morning

12 September, Mackinac Island

For R. M. Pyle

James P. Lenfestey

You settle on the throne
 of the vine, trailing a
string of loud trumpets.

I look up as you open
your prayerful shawl
to the dazzle of morning sun.

A quiet dawn, dew clears
the window glass as
spiders retreat to sleep.

Honeybees buzz your court,
pay respects to your train.

The Sun, holding all
the missing light of the world,
illuminates your wings,
swelling you to a King.

Even the lake, harboring cold
secrets, smooths its furrowed
brow in your presence.
Tomorrow, or the day after,
you will abandon us.
Filled with the nectar of the garden,
You'll drift on high winds
toward the mountains
and forests you remember.

A love story called bigamy,
there and here.
I glance up to tell you
I fear the ending,
beg you to stay.

But you have flown,
jilting even the hummingbird
who came to say good-bye.

Monarch Floats Down From Heaven

25 August, 2020

James P. Lenfestey

Do not read Ray Carver stories if you are sad.
They are so beautiful and sad.

The monarch floats down from heaven
onto the blue flowers. First one, then another,
fuel for the flight back home.

IF I were the monarch, how would I rule?
By doing good with flowers,
taking sweetness, leaving seed?

Or burning myself in the pyre of longing?
Of despair? Fueled by trying, trying,
trying to fix the ruins?

The dawn sun, strong now, rises from the
molten mercury of the lake, late August glare,
drives me inside, where I know not what to be.

Outside, the monarch and the expectant flowers.
Inside, through shades and screens, I hear
them again, the manic leaf blowers,
all day yesterday, and again....

I holster my gun. Which is a rake, which is a gun.
Mount my horse, which is a bicycle,
And ride down to kill them. The blowers
I mean, not the humans earning a living

Disturbing earth's peace. But it is Sunday, after all,
and I was reading this silver morning
stories by Ray Carver, who got what he wanted
out of this life, "even so," he said.

My wife comes down and starts the coffee.
I do not greet her, absorbed in the project
of morning, riding off with my gun
in my holster, my horse gripping the bit
with his nimble lips, answering my touch.

Meanwhile, over the bottom of the Straits
A hundred fifty feet of water flows so subtle no one
sees it, only the nimblest of instruments

can note, one hundred times more movement
in one day than what roars over Niagara Falls,
the same Niagara escarpment I sit on now,
a hundred million years of skeletons and shells.

Nothing I do matters. Nothing I can do will save us,
the monarch, the island, the deep waters.
I will get up from what my fingers tell me
and kiss my wife, who will wonder why.

And when our daughter descends the stairs
to walk her ancient dog, and a visitor comes
to exchange books, poems for me, Ray Carver for him,
the day will begin a new arc, a story.

In which a gentle king still reigns, floating
from generous, forgiving skies,
bearing goodness on his wings.

His coin is silence, his food beauty,
his other love 3000 miles away,
waiting for him, and for spring.

Preserves

Milton J. Bates

I spill a pint of thimbleberries
onto a cookie sheet, then spread
them out to winnow bits of leaf,
the occasional insect or grub.

How many there are, how much alike.
Yet each was chosen from those less ripe
on its nodding stem, each red gem
slipped carefully from its green bezel.

Is this the one I climbed a bank
to harvest? Is that the one
a mosquito made me pay for?

Sugared and simmered in a saucepan,
the berries will shed their shape
and separateness, dissolve into
the anonymity of jam.

I write these words to preserve
not the fruit itself but the picking,
to keep its sweet and tart from getting
lost, like so many sensations,
in the jampot of memory.

Hammock

Taylor Tucker

Rocking gently in a canvas hammock,
watching golden light play on tangled oak boughs
woven into a jungle gym
far above.

I'm not a vampire or a demon or a creature deep beneath the sea,
just a girl who needed a little sun back in her bones.

No clouds and no humidity—
unusual for the typical dog days of late August—
yet still blue sky, the deepest blue
above a plethora of verdant leaves.

Once upon a time, I knew everything.
And then I knew nothing at all.

A robin alights on the worn fence post
and an old dog who's still a toddler
lolls in ecstasy
in the parched grass.

Will my summer fortress still stand in October? I ask the sky, hoping
I'm not about to lose everything I love.

And the azure troposphere gives way
to the incoming rainbow of dusk—
marigold and rose and lavender
cueing the grasshoppers to tune their violins.

Nothing lasts forever, not even this magic
over the earth.

Crickets and cicadas and locusts
begin the familiar evening drone.
Quiet stars, like pearls on a mossy sea bed,
slowly come forth in follow the leader.

No, I can't bottle the wonder of this day. But maybe
I'm a little magic too, and maybe
I can stay.

Embracing

Ellen Schettling Whitehead

High above fir trees
soft beams of morning sunlight
embracing river

Embracing (Boardman River in Grand Traverse County along the North Country Trail) ©*Ellen Schettling Whitehead*

Take Off!

Ellen Schettling Whitehead

Like spokes on a wheel
seeds of a flower with wings
ready for takeoff!

Take Off! (North Country Trail In Kalkaska County)
©Ellen Schettling Whitehead

Cascading

Ellen Schettling Whitehead

Waves of wildflowers
cascading down the hillside
feed both soil and soul

Cascading (Offield Family Viewlands, Harbor Springs)
©Ellen Schettling Whitehead

On The Rediscovery Of My Father-in-Law's Red Schwinn

Glen Young

Most any other year, it would be May, April even,
while this year it is late June, the air summer-
warm, the grass dotted in dandelions, when I
find my way through the old door–hand-fashioned
by a blacksmith who was a grandfather–and into the
family-braille of the musty basement, across the dirt floor
to a second door, then the knot of them, to disentangle
the angle of hand-brakes and fenders, crimped cables,
the spokes still able to turn true enough, the bent basket
and bars to cart and carry me another season, this old
Collegiate from those middle years, before downhills
and downfalls angled him below ground where his people
now largely gather, though their old bikes too still crowd
this basement backroom of the house where we live yet

River Guide

Russell Reece

Sandy at the fly shop books the trips. I pick up the customers just before dawn and haul the boat upstream to the launch. Today it's Jimbo and Ben, two high-rollers from Detroit, clothes and equipment right out of the Orvis catalog. Jimbo's a talker but otherwise they seem okay.

Jimbo asks how long I've been a guide, why I got into the business. I don't tell him that I have to be here, that my soul and the spirt of this place are intertwined. Instead I say, "It's the only money in this bean-can town."

I stow the pop and sandwiches from the 7-Eleven, pick out leaders and flies we'll use today. I have them start with a Coachman and a bead-head dropper. I tie up Jimbo's rig. Ben does his own.

We shove off, Jimbo in front, Ben in the back. I work the oars and keep the boat in the riffles so we can prospect on the way down. We drift by the lodge where a few guys are surrounded in mist, wade-fishing. I get a chill watching them; imagine myself there, cold water rushing by my legs.

My first honey spot is close by, a fast cut along the bank with lots of overhanging branches, always loaded with fish. But another boat's there so we float further downstream and anchor alongside a deep pool.

Ben ties on a Wooley Bugger, casts to the edge of the fast water. He watches the tip of the line, strips in slowly, rod held high, ready to strike. Ben knows what he's doing.

I interrupt Jimbo's monolog and point at a rise near the shore. He lifts his $1200 Winston, makes a few clumsy casts and finishes with a presentation that spooks the trout. Now I've got a bead on these guys it shouldn't be too hard to put them on some fish.

By noon we've drifted 4 miles and both have caught a few. The day is sunny and cool. I pull onto a sandbar under a big white pine where sunlight reflects off the water and glimmers in the branches. I watch the show for a second, feel myself starting to let go but shake it off and break out the sandwiches. We sit in the boat and eat.

They both say they want my job. All my customers want my job. Jimbo offers to invest my money for me. I think about the pile of bills back at the trailer and laugh. I tell him he better get Sandy to book me some more trips.

They get out to pee and I look downstream anticipating the next few hours, the miles of U.P. wilderness, steep cliffs on one side, forest on the other. The spirt is strong here and I could get lost in it. I remind myself to focus, make sure the customers are happy.

We cast off and start the run, flip dries along the edge of the cliff for a mile or so then hit a few good spots on the other side. Jimbo talks the whole time about everything, about nothing. He doesn't have a clue. I watch Ben pause and take things in. I think he's feeling it a little and I'm happy about that.

We catch a few more fish, snap lots of pictures, big smiles. We hit the take-out point by the fly-shop around 4:30.

I hate coming off, but Sandy's got the trailer waiting and Jimbo and Ben are tired. I pull the boat in and help them with their gear. They give me a nice tip, say they'll ask for me the next time they fish here. Sandy likes that. Jimbo tries his cell phone, curses the lack of a connection. Ben takes another long look at the river, gives me a nod.

No customers tomorrow so I'll be on my own. I'll launch the boat, float the river, take it slow, fish for a while. Maybe not. It'll depend. Tomorrow could be the day when the spirit will take me. I'll let go and be gone.

Lily Pads On Brocky Lake ©*Lisa Fosmo*

Ode To My Bicycle

Philip Rice

Da Vinci would have swooned
at the sheer simplicity:
two wheels and a chain;
wild to think
they only figured that out
a century ago.

Delicate frame
like a damselfly's body
wheel spokes webbed
like cicada wings
or the orb web
of a diligent, tiny
spider in the garden
at dawn
after a gentle rain.

My feet mere inches
from the pavement,
hover above the road
as a hummingbird hovers
above summer blossoms,
always thirty minutes
from starvation.

A human miracle:
the bicycle!
Its engine
is my body
fueled by escargot,
brussels sprouts,
creme brûlée, wine,
and the sheer joy
of chasing a sunset.

Mulligan I

Christine Saari

After breaking through the gorge
the Mulligan meanders southward
toward the Dead River.

Escarpments rise out of the valley
on both sides of the stream.
Wild trout play in the Rocking Chair Lakes.

Beavers build their lodges in the Mulligan.
Wetlands and isolation have spared
a stand of virgin white pine.

Logging companies have clear-cut the forest floor,
left behind debris, scarred the valley,
yet gifted us with a view of the escarpment.

Four-wheelers buzz on dusty roads.
On Silver Lake the roar of motorboats
drowns out the call of the loon.

When darkness falls and stillness descends,
the big dipper stands guard above the waters.
A multitude of stars glimmer in the night sky.

We hear the faint boom of underground blasts
and the glow from the new mine lightens the horizon.
Nonetheless, this place remains our refuge.

Worst Comes To Worst

Tara Vancil

If the worst ever comes,
I'll run.
Racing to the trees
to find the best.

In me I find high hopes.
No,
that's just those trees.
A pure heart.
The water washed it clean.
Clear mind.
It'll muddy itself,
given the chance.

The best finally shows,
stumbling onto broken glass.

Who left that bottle way out here?
The worst.

Great Blue Heron – DeYoung Nature Preserve ©*Susan Kirt*

Blue Racer

—Coluber constrictor foxii

Greg Rappleye

To kill a snake is still to have a snake.
Joan Didion

I saw a blue racer
flickering through the candleweed, and wanting it—
cream belly and cobalt flanks,
a darting tongue with quick tip—
I snatched it as a raptor might:
blue dazzler, eyed once and swept high.
I placed it in a wooden box
[the "fastest snake" astonished, writhing],
and laid the box among the wheels
blocked high beneath a stripped-out Nash.
And there, the serpent would not calm,
wanting only dew on its quick-tipped tongue,
wanting to be gone. It was a wicked sin
to keep a racer boxed beneath a salvage wreck.
But those were days of wanton needs;
of covetousness. Each morning,
beguiled by the electric blue,
greedy for its coiling, for its cold blink
as I cracked the box to sunlight,
for the snake's power, alive and sly
beneath the wretched Nash, to make Mam curse
in her whiskey-addled tongue;

all this consoled me into August,
until I found the box shattered
and the snake tossed among the Queen Anne's lace,
hacked to cream and cobalt pieces.
Its head was stepped flat
as foretold, and there was that scythe—
wet blade plunged into sand.
Who killed the blue racer?
Not I, not even in an angry boy's dream,
though I'd slept fitfully that night,
though there'd been a stalking moon
and a man whistling high through the tall pines,
though the book said a troublesome child
would stir and stir, causing the serpent's death.
And oh, the blow flies got on with it—
that grievous sipping; their cutty little tongues.
So eagerly they buzzed
at their long-anointed tasks.

Almost Dark

Paul Maxbauer

In summer during a warm spell, near the end of the day,
the big trout come out from hiding. They move out from

undercut banks, log jams and deep holes, they swim to
shallower water, on the lookout for insects, minnows,

crayfish and mice. Bats appear, fluttering over the river
from tree to tree, feeding on mosquitoes, caddis, and mayflies.

They can have all the mosquitoes they want for all I care,
and black flies that bite along the forehead and around the

ears, they are especially welcome to have them all.
But I hope they spare the fireflies, little flashes of light

dancing midair in the darkening woods, illuminating the
border between forest and meadow, the river and its

cedar-lined banks, filling me with heightened expectancy for
a good hatch and rising trout, and reminding me of blinking

lights strung outside of homes at Christmas time.
Other creatures come out. Mink, muskrats and beaver swim

along the riverbank, deer come in the evening to take a
drink, large owls perch in treetops, and hoot. Once one

swooped close overhead, giving me a shiver with the whoosh
of its long wings. But it is those big trout I am most interested in,

after sunset when streaks of yellow, orange, and pink paint the western sky, and the surface of the river takes on a silvery glow.

Seeing a trout take a mayfly on the surface with an audible slurp, leaving a large ring on the water, quickens the blood,

and gets my full attention. That vision and the murmur of the river keeps me up at night.

Surveilling Channel Ghosts ©*Michele Austin*

An Invitation From The Wood

Gabriel Wilder

The bird spoke to me
Please. Please. Take a seat among the fire lit leaves.
The wind and the trees are about to begin the greatest dance of the wood.
Oh, witness the fervor in their movement. The intensity, the passion.
The ecstasy that radiates from the perfection of this partnership.
It is nothing other than delightful. Yes indeed!
I guarantee that your heart will be seized by all its beauty.
And after their performance, come lend an ear to the birds. The greatest orators in all the wood.
Listen in, there are so many willing to speak.
Robins who have journeyed to faraway lands.
Gulls who have conquered rolling storms.
Their eloquent details will arrest the wandering mind.
And as the sun takes its leave the entertainment does not stop.
You will be entranced by the flickering of light in the space of night.
It'll make you wonder if fairies are real.
Be wary of the chants of death by the bats who are hungry.
Heed the gossip of the coyotes as they know all that happens under the moon.
The violence, the vice, the mystery of the night, will bring forth the vigor hidden in complacent hearts.
Please. Please. Take a seat.
The wood is about to wake, and you will see it in all its glory.

Loon Feeding Young – Cedar Lake ©*Susan Kirt*

Field Study

Skip Renker

One of the birds at a busy feeder
will likely die today, the bird behavior
guidebook says, citing field studies—
maybe the beautiful but tyrannical
blue jay, scaring off chickadees
and scattering sunflower seeds,
or the trunk-spiraling nuthatch, so quick
and seemingly cheery, or the mourning dove,
plump and slow, bait for the red-tailed hawk.

Why fly? Why labor to eat
half your weight every day? I pause
in these human ruminations
to watch the angular egret,
breathtaking in her singular focus
as she stalks the sunlit shallows on legs
that evolved over millions of years—
they lift and fall in slow deliberation,
her beak stabs like a piston
in and out of the river we've not yet

ruined. How is it that beauty
suffuses these systems
of transformation, this eating and killing
and excreting and being eaten?
The river's teeming with food,
shining ripples moving slowly
above darker, colder currents.

Michigan Calling

Skip Renker

Horse-traders, railroaders, frock-coated
sharpies—wheeler-dealers stole
or wheedled most of our woods
and waters from the Algonquians,
then frontier legislators put quill pens
to paper, drew straight or squiggly
lines, rigged the borders of our
two peninsulas, boundaries unheeded
by migratory snow buntings, grey wolves,
any river swimmer or burrowing
woodchuck. Still, I feel a deep allegiance

to the waterfalls, loblolly pines,
and Porcupine Mountains of our north country,
and to this southern mitten shape, the bluffs
and harbors of our lake-length shores,
to the baseball team of my youth and age,
and to our Motor City. Some call us
Michiganians, but I prefer
Michiganders, the humble whimsy
of honkers on the wing, though
no glacier ever stopped
at a state line, or, retreating,
gouged a mind-made word.

Sunset on Brocky Lake ©*Lisa Fosmo*

Framed In Blue

...for Guss Lord

Ellen Lord

I remember a spring morning
at my grandparent's house in Trout Creek.
It was a logging town, always so much to do.
I am awakened by the aroma of coffee and bacon
as sunlight stammers the trees beyond my window.
Grandma is making breakfast.

Fast forward 60 years; it's almost a ghost town.
The ancestors' photos adorn the walls.
I lay awake in the same room; the aroma of lilacs
mingles with the silence of an empty house.
I wonder, what can I fall in love with today?

If you travel Highway 28 west of town
look for the '*Agate Falls*' sign. It's easy to miss.
There will be a rustic park nestled near the East Branch
of the Ontonagon River. A boardwalk leads to an overlook
but you will want to go further, deeper into the wild.
Look for a deer trail in the tangle of forest then follow
the river down...all the way down to the falls.

Be brave...for the path will be rocky and steep.
You will hear the waterfalls before you see them—
listen as the river crescendos into pools of prismed mist.
Climb onto outcrops of stone as sunglow spangles
the pinewoods. Just you and the ghosts of old fishermen
casting for rainbow trout, framed in blue.

Voice Of A Firefly

John Lennon

Smoke stretching towards stars
In companionable silence
With the noises of a forest,
Alone, louder
Than usual.
This is the voice of a firefly,
Calling those with
Open hearts
To the last nights of summer.

Youth In Summer

John Lennon
(written with Nick Ender)

Dancing carside under a broken sign
Our bodies turned like moonlit engines.
Neon cut the tension of the summer night
And painted us in cold rainbows.

We pay homage in fever dreams
To the beat of the radio and
Toss bottles against the wall of tomorrow.

Take time
Blacked out on blissful youth
And notice how the stars
Will never look again.

In Search Of The Essential *©Laura Story Johnson*

Vigils On Old Mission

Bonnie Dankert

As I reconnect with each pause of stillness,
In the midst of lapping water's voices,
I drift into a reverie of an early morning
paddle along the western shore of Grand Traverse Bay.

Gathering wet rocks into pockets,
I study stately silhouettes of an Evergreen forest—greet
a canopy of Sugar Maples and Red Oaks, offer my homage to Blue Spruce,
Northern White Cedar, Hemlock, White Pine and Paper Birch.

As Goldfinches flit amidst green Winterberry with striking fruit
of red and yellow, a Cardinal calls to his mate at dawn.
A kaleidoscope of blues blend into deeper depths of the bay,
likened to an azure flash of Eastern Bluebirds
swooping up in unison to meet this new day.

Breath by breath, step by step, an abiding solace
is offered from this vivid landscape. Beauty's integrity
reveals a passing wisdom.

When darkness falls, a grand finale unfolds,
vast scatters of stars spill across the northern sky
with Venus and Jupiter joining the Moon's full glow.

Suddenly, calls from a pair of loons echo off
The banks of Power Island as I hold my breath to listen.

These enduring mysteries restore reverence to all I call this life.

Fungus Family ©*Karen Walker*

Karen
Walker

Halfway Home (Stuck In The Middle)

Charles Rammelkamp

I always thought it was cool
the lighthouse at the tip
of Old Mission Peninsula stood
halfway between the Equator and the North Pole,
midway between tropical and frozen,
a sign in front of the lighthouse proclaiming
proclaiming the fact: as symbolic
as Neil Armstrong's flag stuck on the Moon.

The Forty-fifth parallel—
not so unique, after all, considering
the size of the Earth:
How many places can stake the same claim?
Minneapolis, for one, at the same latitude.
But here it seemed like a bull's eye,
at the edge of land, the lip of the lake,
where the bay ended and the big water began,
the lighthouse there to orient ships.

So of course, every summer,
I had to have my picture taken
in front of the sign, right?
Kilroy was here!

Stuck Record

Raymond Luczak

A cottony silence drapes itself over the tops of trees already losing its summer abundance. Soon the winds will tap the branches again and again to ferret out the weaker leaves. The rising steam unleashes pearls that evaporate too quickly before the oysters of the day can snap them up dry. The sun has no way of breaking through the vaulted walls of grip. The slight chill that blemishes the landscape of memory into a flat whiteness with jags of black and gray and brown is a stuck record. The needle of time keeps skipping *uh-huh uh-huh, so here we are.*

Under The Boughs Of Cedar

Shelley Smithson

Under the boughs of cedar
camphor scent hangs in the air
like dripping honey.
From inside this nestled perch,
formed in the cradle of trunks,
I see glimmers of radiant sun
tiptoe on the water's surface.
Through the web of cedar sprays,
I follow the crooning seagull,
aloft in undulating flight.
It rises in currents of wind
that carry all hope and all silence
over the ripples of land and bay,
letting sorrow
soften into the folds of my heart.

Looking For Someone

Patrice Trentacoste

Some say crows are bad omens. In the rangy Hemlock outside Raila Batiste's window is a particularly fierce-looking one squawking something awful. Poking a fingernail at the screen, she yells, "Quit trying to scare me, Bird. I'm going fishing with Willie tonight no matter what you say."

On Tuesdays Willie, her beautiful boy, her grandson, always meets her on the banks of the Ontonagon River after his shift at Effie's, where he mans the fryer, same as he's been doing since he was thirteen. He ought to be living a larger life. She knows this and suspects he does too, because only last week, he'd said his Yooper life was pointless.

"Ooof," she'd scoffed. "What are you talking about?

Shrugging, he'd grabbed a sausage sandwich, dripped sauce on the floor, patted her head, "Have a good day, Gram," and left without shutting the back door. Still, she's glad for his company. Boy, is she ever. Two years ago, her husband died, and shortly after that, her daughter, Willie's mother, ran off with an Aleutian scholar to study otters. So as far as she's concerned, Willie can slop sauce or whatever he wants, so long as he keeps living with her. So long as they have their Tuesday nights.

Slipping into her moccasins, Raila scuffs down the hall. "What's this?" There's a post-it on the pantry door from Willie. *I 'll be late. Need to talk. Something huge. Prepare yourself.* 😌 *W.*

That kid—always signing post-its with funny little drawings. His sense of *yoomer,* he calls it. Prepare herself. Whatever for. A girlfriend. Wouldn't that be grand. Well, there's no sense worrying about what "huge" might mean to a twenty-two-year-old stuck in a loop.

For pity's sake. The crow's going berserk again. She bangs open the porch door and tosses some fresh berries onto the lawn. Maybe that will shut it up. After sitting in the Sauna till she's beet red and prune-y, she reads a novel in the hollow of her forest, wearing nothing but a giant orange striped beach towel, encircled by yellow coreopsis and pink zinnias. During the Wheel of Fortune, she pins her best flies onto her shirt pocket and glances out the window. At last, the sky is lowering for dusk. It is time to go, although it won't be long before the error in her thinking shows itself, because crows do know their business.

Her stride is long, like a man's. Beyond her little woods are the knotweed and spongy sphagnum beds and beyond that, cedar swamps and a bunch of copper-mine ruins. Those she skirts widely, they're treacherous this time of night. Deeper and deeper into the forest she goes, her daypack clanking with goods: water filter, coffee, a mini cookstove, collapsible cool pack for the fish, homemade jerky, made by Willie actually, a military grade whistle, and Willie's note, so they can discuss it fully while pinching nightcrawlers and spinners. He will smell of beeswax and stout. He will sling an arm around her shoulders and whisper, "I'll never quit fishing with *you*, Gram." Willie is her main man now.

But her love dream is wrecked by a whiff of cigarette smoke. Site-poachers? Picturing the Bassmaster reels she keeps hidden under a tree, she picks-up speed but stops on second thought when she reaches the Great Eastern Pine. It's their talking tree. At its base is a pile of stones. Rearranging them, she builds a small cairn in the arrangement of a warning, *Keep sharp,* just in case. Stones in a circle mean, *Hoot when you're in earshot.* She places them prominently, not wanting to be surprised by him or any other two-leggeds in the dark, and hikes on, stomp, stomp, clank, clank, her thick white braid dampening in the cold dew.

Finally, there's the familiar smell of sulfurous mud. "I'm here," she calls to the river. "Give up your fish and show me a good time." What was she thinking, leaving those stupid stones. She inhales deeply just to be sure. No, no tobacco whatsoever. Throwing her head back, she yells, "Caw, caw!" Then once more, "Caw!" Where's that dumb bird when you want to laugh in its face?

Because she is looking up instead of down, she does not see the low branch straddling two rocks and cries out as she stumbles into the shallow ravine, she and Willie use as their work-pit.

Out from under the leaden sunset comes a square-shaped man, unlit cigarette in his teeth. "Whoa, you okay, Missus? Take it easy. Lemme give you a hand!" But he isn't giving her a hand, he's lighting up.

Rubbing her knees, she glares at him."Where'd *you* come from?" tucking-in her blouse roughly.

"Pardon me?" The man waves-in a second one who skids down some switchbacks, his wits frayed like pointy little strings come loose of their bindings. Clodhoppers. The closest is short-statured, pale and wearing stiff new camo head to toe. There's a bunch of gold chains around his neck. Flattening a lumpy pocket, he fumbles for his smokes, puts a spare over his ear, and eyes the trail front and back, then stares at Rai, as if she's the one who should explain herself.

"You put that branch there," she accuses.

"No, ma'am, we did not."

"Liars." Her blanket skirt is torn where her boot gouged the hem. "That branch don't belong there. See? It's been propped up. You after my spot, with this whole wide woods to choose from?"

Rummaging in her pack, she takes a swig of water to slow her anger. She doesn't care for these two; they've ignored the wilderness code: *don't crowd the angler who gets there first.* Also, when you're accosted—or whatever this is—and you're an old doll-baby, it's best, she has learned, to appear ornery, so no one thinks they can get a jump on you.

The pasty fellow inhales so long and deeply, she holds her breath too. Finally, spitting a nick of tobacco from the tip of his too-pink tongue, he clambers down the ditch, his fishing vest swinging unevenly, takes her by the arm. His manner is gentle enough but insistent. Back on level ground, she yanks free, feeling her pack peeling away from her shoulders. *What in the world?*

Velcro scratching, the guy fondles each zipper and flaps and says, as if speaking to a child, "We aren't going to hurt you, Ma'am," which is a sure sign they are. Willie's note is fished-out and read aloud as the guy glances at his pal who nods back at him.

His drawl is so slow and soft, she has to tip her ear towards him. "Truth is, we're lookin' for someone."

"'*Looking* for someone?'" she repeats.

"That's right. We're…we're investigators. I'm Emmons. This here's Neil Bovee."

"Cops?" She can't believe it.

"No, not cops. Apologize to Missus, Neil."

Neil Bovee says the log over the rocks was a mistake. It was supposed to be a landmark. He messed-up, is all.

Emmons explains, "We're fugitive recovery agents and we got us a missing perp."

"A what?" Their words are crazy. *Missing perp.* TV hooey.

"Well, let me tell it, now!" he gestures with his cigarette. "We're after a bail-cutter." Her pack is handed back to her almost gallantly. He tells Bovee she has no phone and can't warn nobody. "Here's the thing. You listening?"

Of course, she's listening, what do they think.

"The guy we're after beat up a woman. Badly."

"That's horrible," Rai says genuinely, "really awful, but what does it have to do with me? I haven't come across anybody like that."

"Tell her," the bigger one says.

"It has to do with *you,* Ma'am, because the guy we're after is your grandson, William."

She stares at them, first at the stumpy one, then at the guy with tattoos on his fingers. "Well, here's a newsflash for you boys. I don't have a grandson!" her mind reeling to that girl from a year ago—the one who'd dumped him the minute her ex was back. It had been a bad break-up, as she recalls. Inside her canvas sack, Raila's pots are trembling like bones in boiling soup.

"Excuse me, Lady, but you're the liar. I read the note." Emmons spits into the sandy soil. A drop hits her cheek.

She wipes the moisture away, pretending it didn't happen and they aren't there, that Willie is there instead, with his yoomer and a fistful of nightcrawlers.

"Fact is, he admitted all of it at some bar. *Effie's*. Said he was going off-grid tonight after hanging out with the best angler he knows. Folks there knew who he meant and which trailhead he uses too."

The other one, Neil, for the first time, reveals a mouthful of tiny pearly teeth.

"Got any proof?" she thinks to ask.

Shivering against nightfall, the man withdraws a laminated authorization card. "We work for a bail bondsman."

Darned if there isn't an agent's badge clipped to the leather flap of his wallet. This is no prank. But what *is* it. Willie would never—

"We bring in runners. This case here, the facts add up. We been tracking you a ways. That's your gear-stash. No?"

The fellow is alarmingly flat, official on the outside but something else festering inside. As if to confirm her suspicions, he rolls his wrist against his jacket cuff, almost spastically then returns the card to his wallet and his wallet to his pocket, twitchy-like.

"We ain't cops. But make no mistake, we have authority—all the way to the Wisconsin border."

Sweeping his hand in a circle, he adds in a snottier tone, "You best cooperate. When you expect him?" Now he's taking a draw from a mega-caffeine drink and swallowing loose pills from a pocket. Bingo.

When a small shiny creature jiggles inside a run-off puddle, Bovee jumps off a big rock where he's apparently been trying to get a cellphone signal, pivots his heel and grinds it flat. It is a Michigan painted turtle and it's bleeding-out like a squashed tomato.

Shrieking, Raila drops to the ground and waves her hands over the murdered creature.

"I didn't know what it was," Bovee half-whines, dragging his shoe through the muck to wash off the mess, shoving his useless phone back in his pocket.

Raila balls-up her fists behind her back and longs for the river. It is there. Just behind the aspens, lapping and churning with speckled beauties. All she wants to do is go fishing. Can't she just go fishing? When she gets really stressed, really scared, she tends to laugh, and does so now, but without sound, contorting her face.

Emmons quits scratching and sighs. "What's gonna happen now is, we're gonna make a fire, so things look ordinary when William gets here. We don't wanna spook him," thumbing at Bovee.

"Get kindling." As the turtle-killer lumbers off, Emmons' unfriendly stare reminds Rai of what the locals say over at Effie's. They say, bounty hunters can carry and enter property without search warrants. Maybe that's how you catch creeps who beat-up women. The thought of it sickens her. But so does another one.

A couple weeks back, Willie had gone to a job-fair, over to the far side of the peninsula and stayed longer because of car trouble. That's what he'd said, and it made sense at the time. What if….She can't even think about it.

Back with dry twigs, Bovee squats to put a butane to the tinder. On his lower back is another tattoo, a crimson poppy wrapped around the Earth, the word *Free* spanning the equator. It is rather beautiful. Ironic, given his career choice. The wood ignites crisply.

"This here fire's fine for now," Emmons says. "He won't be suspicious. Once here, he'll wanna go quietly *for your sake*."

Clearly, they've seen through her lie. For good or ill, Willie is her grandson and they know it. She massages her palm with her thumb, feeling frightened, deeply, intensely frightened.

As darkness falls, the forest loses definition, and the only constant is the river passing over low boulders. In the firelight, she spots an ugly rash creeping up Emmons' arm. It looks like half his face is swollen too. Poison Ivy. Fine by her.

After a spell of fire-watching and listening to the night sounds, she hears a piercing Willie-inflected hoot. *He is here. My beautiful boy. He'll have read the stones. He'll save me and give these dopes the slip.* Turning nice-and-easy to the lawmen and parting her teeth gruesomely, she reveals green slime from the shoot she's been chewing and says, sweetly, "Fresh ash and spit from bamboo grass, if you want it. For your rash. Old Ojibwe remedy. You've been in the poison-leaf, you know."

Bovee looks from Emmons to her recoiling at both of them, screws up his face and says, "Don't get cute, Missus. This is serious business." But they both know he's Emmon's flunkey, Emmons, the man now painfully involved with his flesh. The worst is around his wrist. Grimacing and shaking his head, he snatches a long branch, scrabbles to his feet and stands over Rai. Whack. The switch strikes a rock so fiercely, it breaks, and twigs land in her lap, one on her shoulder.

She gasps. "Hey, what are you?"

Dropping the branch, he pulls out a 9 mm pistol and fires a round over her shoulder.

Bovee hollers in protest.

"Get up," Emmons waves his enflamed gun hand.

The ground is hard. She is old. She'd forgotten about guns, even though she'd noticed that bulging vest a half-dozen-times. She just hadn't gone far enough in her thinking to account for what she'd seen. The presence of the gun is a horror to her, a horror.

"Put out that fire," Emmons barks to Bovee, who now seems as mixed up as she is. "Take us to where y'all live, Lady. He's not here, so, we'll get him there. Settle this. It'll go easier for him this way. I got a compass." He shimmies his gold chains so she can see the clunky thing.

"Alright, I'll take you. Put that dumb gun away!"

When Bovee kicks sand over the fire, the blackness is blinding. To read the ground, you have to know how flashlight beams hit sharp edges differently than softer soils, knowledge these two lack. For a moment, she stares at her captors without budging. One looms over her like a tree, the other, like an albino hound, and she realizes what has just happened. She can take them to the cabin or *anywhere she wants.* If only Willie will stay back and not rush them. Slowly, she begins leading the men toward the mines.

Torches bouncing along the trail, the three of them rustle through the crude paths. When a second owl-screech sets off a coyote, Bovee hisses, "How come we're not goin' out the way we come in?"

Emmons merely thumbs the hollow of his eye and twitches his gun hand. Every couple yards he gags on his own cigarette smoke. Their desperation is real. Freelancers don't get paid when they don't get their man.

In that sickly tone of his, Emmons says, "Don't much matter. If it *is* the wrong way, no one will find the old thing for months," gesturing to *her* and waving the gun at Bovee, directing him to keep their formation tight. "Old Thing," he sneers, stretching his neck till he looks like the dead turtle. Then, skipping erratically, he shoves Bovee to the side and waves the gun in the air like a fool, yelling, "Yah!" Guzzles more caffeine.

Bovee looks at her with weak eyes and she knows it's up to her to do what must be done.

Nearby, where the trail crisscrosses a defunct railroad track, there's a snarl of barbed wire, some weathered boards. Most of the remaining uncapped shafts are nothing but shallow pits, full of porcupine pellets and fox piss, but deep enough to snare the unsuspecting. It's all she'll need to slow them down and escape. A wild onion odor laced with mint rises off the earth. Its pungency enlivens her until the next gun blast sears the sky.

Wheeling about, she screams into their faces. They freeze like rodents and it's all the time she needs to drop her pack and flee into the curtain of darkness, half expecting to be shot at. Not more than thirty yards out though, she hears a very different-sounding commotion, that of breaking boards and only then, gunshot. Someone cries out in pain. The cry is not Willie's.

Against all common sense, Rai reverses herself and finds Bovee crumpled over an opening in the ground and Emmons trapped beneath him, straddling a hole and sagging under the bigger man's weight. Bovee's the one shot. They look like a woodpile with flashing eyes. There's a flailing hand. Then up-ending boots. More yelling and choking. Then, crack. The earth gives way, and they are gone.

It's as if they never existed!

Crouching over the shaft, her hands sinking into the peat, she can't see a thing. "Why'd you bring that gun?" she yells.

Are they dead? She listens. Nothing. The sky spins dizzily. What is happening. Wait, is that....Yes, there's a faint keening coming from the hole, followed by muffled voices and the smell of something burning. Down in the belly of the ruin, Emmons' has lit a cigarette. Thank God.

"I'm going for help!" she yells, her voice a sob. "Hang on. Just hang on!" After hanging her blanket skirt over a tree limb as a marker, she blows her mighty whistle in every direction, throttling her own ears while crying, "Willie. Willie. Willie!" Her whistle peals. But Willie is not out there. He isn't anywhere. The hoots were not his. If he *were* out there, he'd have shown himself long ago. He's on the run, is where he is.

Fixing on a slurry of gray incandescence in the sky, she heads in its direction, pretty sure it's the spotlight on the tavern's peaked roof. In the dark, a lone light can shine for miles.

The forest parts for her and Mars' red flicker guides her. After all, this is her territory, her river land. Her boot prints are on every deer trail. Sealed in its gauzy leaves are her daydreams. Inside these swampy woods, she's been a tree-climber, a sky-reader and a minnow-catcher, and has lived off its spirit her whole life. She knows exactly where she is. At last, there's a glint of road paint. Flashlight waving, she flags a driver who agrees to take her to town.

Effie's is empty. Frowning and sliding a cellphone across the bar top, Effie places a shot-glass of vodka and a tumbler of ice water in front of Rai. The dispatcher in the Sheriff's office confirms that a pair of bounty hunters had registered there that morning. Hearing how aggressive they'd been, how one even fired his weapon, he asks if she wants to file a complaint. She has the right.

"No, don't believe I do, no. But," she inhales quaveringly and tells him the rest. "They fell in. Not too deep, but deep enough. Over by the mines. They're in bad trouble. One of them accidentally shot the other." She says nothing about her Willie. Not one word. And neither does he.

"We'll handle it from here," he says and promises to retrieve her eagle blanket.

She tries Willie's prepay. No connection. What a surprise.

Effie's magenta fingernail is tapping the side of the water tumbler and her attention is on the TV screen over the bar. Without facing Rai, she says something remarkable in its clarity. "Rai, honey, if you're expecting Willie tonight, forget it. He left. Said something about, oh, wait, stupid me. Here.

"He left this for you. Him and his notes. Said to give it to you when you came by with your catch. Didn't even work his second shift. Cashed his check and off he gone. That's how it is with kids, eh. Though, if you ask me, he's got a lot of his mother in..." stopping when Rai grabs the paper from her.

With a trembling thumb, Raila unfolds the note.

Gram, St. Ignace called back. Job at hotel in AM. Benefits. Sorry to stand you up. Hope U R OK. It's all good. ⊕ W.

Willie is safe. Numbly, she rolls the note into a tiny cylinder and munches absently on a pretzel while staring at the TV. The sound is muted and tickertape-news is running across the bottom with the name, William Skidmore. Apparently, Skidmore was arrested at a gas station in Ironwood where the U.P. connects with Wisconsin. Assault and battery against a onetime girlfriend.

"Hey, that guy was in here today," Effie grows excited. Then her hand flies to her mouth. "There was two other strangers in here after. Dudes coming and going. I told them about the other one, how he was running his mouth. Jackass."

Effie slumps onto the stool next to Rai, almost as an afterthought, adding, "I think they heard me talking about *our* Willie in the bargain, you know. How *he* was leaving the area, wishing *he* could, you know, go fishing with *you* one last time. I think they mixed up the names." With one eye squeezed closed, the opened one quivering, she turns squarely to Rai. "I didn't know better, Rai. They the ones out there. In those pit-holes by the swamps. Serves 'em right. Huh, two Willies, who'd have thought?"

She should feel elated. Blouse bunched in her hand so tightly she can't open her lungs, she tries to swallow the pretzel in her mouth, but it tastes like wet sand and won't go down. She spits it into a napkin, repulsed by the trace of bamboo grass, and even more by how she'd misread Willie's heart. At the very least, she should have confirmed the last name. How did no one think to mention it.

Effie locks up and drives Raila home, Raila unable to stop crying the entire time. Beneath the hemlock, stars are winking in and out of the browned-out appendages. She has no intention of going inside the house until she gets word about Emmons and Bovee and crawls instead under the picnic table behind the sauna shed where she lies on her back on the clean dirt. There are no skeeters, the breeze has stilled. After a while, she turns on her side, uses her arm as a pillow, and tucks the other hand between her knees and falls into uneasy dreams.

The next day her landline rings. The fugitive hunters are being treated at the local hospital, and they're said to be full of apologies. Should she take them some homemade pasties? she wonders. Be her higher self. Nah.

Finally, Willie calls, sending his love, regretting that he won't be home anytime soon. The following Tuesday night, she heads for the Ontonagon. The river is her main man now.

Tanka Trilogy

Ellen Lord

I

Forest Bathing

Soft fascination
interplay of leaves and light.
Let your mind wander
into the aspen's branches.
Splendor of dappled beauty.

To flow unfurled
raptor rides the solar wind.
Follow, just follow.
Bird song echoes in the mist.
Spring dreams radiate with dawn.

Unfettered hours
pulsate in primitive song.
Breathe into the sky's
kaleidoscope of color
humbled by the mystery.

II

Spring Equinox

Equal dark and light
revel in the breath of spring.
Blossoms on pearwood
swell with their pregnant promise.
Sun and moon adorn the sky.

Anticipation
finds us eager to enter
earth's return to green
a soft transcendent knowing
the wisdom of middle ground.

Wax and wane of days
this cycle of existence.
We stand in-between
to flow with the pulse of now
our own zenith and nadir.

III

Yearn

"If anyone understood loneliness,
the moon would." (Kaya)

Try to touch the wind.
Dark eyes search far-fleeting clouds.
Try to hold the rain.
Why does the mockingbird sing?
Desire lingers at dusk.

Wait like a perched bird
anchored in a high-sway wind
longing to depart
yet reluctant to let go
no mate to compass her home.

Why is it that you
yearn to marry the nightbird?
Unrequited muse.
Watchful orb of the wolf moon
waxes, then wanes in your eyes.

Lumberjack Tango

Ellen Lord

Dance with me
make me sway
kiss me on the lips.

How tall are you?

Bend me into your dreams
let's shimmy, shimmy along
well beyond midnight.

Let me wear your hat.

My Refuge *©Moon Seagren*

Homestead

CJ Giroux

Under a sagging roof and escaping western winds,
I grasp splintered rails of weakening wood

and pull myself past missing rungs
into the streaked light of the barn's loft.

Taking the pulse of wasps' nests—half hoping for humming—
I clear straw, spiders' strands from spirit holes.

I look for the big lake, a salve out of sight,
beyond the snaking road, past orchard and order,

but nearer, where field meets fir, where cornstalks cut
like broken glass, I see only melting snow

sought by wild turkeys in furrowed ground;
startled by sounds I can't hear, these black-brown bodies still,

so too the sentinel buck, sniffing for danger,
in morning's red glow. Contemplating movement, flight, ascent,

I seek beating wings, Jacob's ladder, but find,
in swallows' homes, only the stray feather, cracked cups crumbling.

First Fall

Milton J. Bates

Soon the maple leaves will crash
and burn, their red and orange flames
lighting up rain-blackened roads.
The trees will turn to skeletons.

But first the white pines must shed
their yearly crop of yellow
needles. Five-strawed whisks carpet
our yard, brightening dead stalks
of bee balm and black-eyed Susan.

Some tick against the window
coming down, then link with others
on our deck to spell out cryptic
messages in Viking runes.

Tell us your secret, great pines.
How can you spend all that gold,
yet remain so green and glossy?

Dead Pine In Dead River *©Milton J. Bates*

Protar's Tomb

Joseph Slaney

For honor and bravery
and the myths of the fiefdom,
cannon fire and heraldry
in each and every kingdom.

And in a woods far away,
rests a man kind and modest,
whom birds, at the break of day,
praise in song bright and honest

Palmer's Two-Step

Joseph Slaney

At a pitchy piano,
squeaky, snappish and twangy,
weaving rhythms staccato,
brilliant, agile, and rangy.

The left hand drives steadily
the cadenced, muffled baseline.
The right scatters melody,
showering notes like starshine.

To a twinkling crescendo,
the sharp ivories ascend,
pushing the beat allegro
before swiftly they descend,

while round the hall nosily
whooping, prancing, and quicksteps,
islanders dance joyfully
to Edward Palmer's Two-Step.

On The Docks

S.D. Dillon

A freighter cuts through the channel. I follow
the smell of barnacles, zebra mussels crusted on the hull,
north-northwest, some remote corner to Lake Michigan.
The deck fumes diesel and small mouth.
I am there and I am here. In the waves,
in the mounds of trees onshore, a diamond winks back:
On the Grand Traverse beach, the crinkle of sun-bleached fish,
tangled on copper and Antrim shale,
eases with a wash over my feet, and a nip:
I pluck a crawfish from my Achilles,
raise him by the trembling thorax.
He throws back his claws in supplication, flailing at the clement sky
for something to wisp him away.
Facing Leelanau, I wade ankle-deep, where I know it's still too close—
just moments until another crest would beach the crustacean,
abandoning him to sun and birds.
Waist-deep, I let him down in a calm.
Back here on the dock, I stare out at an edge
we stumble over into sky, and, beyond that—

The Old Masters

S.D. Dillon

The bog boils, an acrylic broth.
Flax ferments like turpentine,
cabbage, whiskey,
frogs an injection clouding the water.

I am running with a net by a pond in Petoskey,
swoop over a toad
and cusp him in my hand.
The membrane draws
From over his eyes.
I feel the pulse
of his breath, the flare
of nostrils,
and set him on the shore.
He skims through algae into muck and rocks.

At the fatal noise, the naturalist departs—
I remain, scanning my knuckles, fingers, palms,
hands of some painter or surgeon,
fit for a pen or hazel stick,
writhing amidst these amphibians like being flayed,
gesturing forth:
the sound
of Icarus' tiny scream.

Bare Back

Phillip Sterling

"How blessed horses smell in this bitter world."
—Jim Harrison

Something in August fog
wants a horse, these odors
of cabbage, piss and vinegar,
the inception of love

                                        Step into it:
let your skin chortle with delight
the mare chuckle softly
at your nerve
                                        as if air

were nothing more than laughter
at morning's expense

Oxymoron

Phillip Sterling

What thought this light
clustering the surface
of our nameless creek
like a shimmering

of bees, tensile and
sparkling, a swarm so
brilliant as to be both
threat and elation,

difficult to look at
for any length of time,
our downcast eyes
unaccustomed to

the sun's disregard
for silt or clarity, depth
or dimension. Here is
spring surfacing.

Here are the words

I love you

shimmering the surface
of a language I learned
long ago (from you,

who loved me) and
from which light gleams
so infrequently
we are startled by it.

The Cormorant

Taylor Tucker

I found a cormorant,
very dead,
washed up among the rocks
on the shoreline midmorning.

The night before,
a rock out of place
as I scanned the line, my nightly practice,
looking for discrepancies.

In the light of day, that shape,
no stone at all, but a heavy black bird
lying on his back
partially submerged.

Climbing down the bank to retrieve him, I found
that the gentle September air had rotted out his breast,
yet below the waterline, in growing chill,
he lay intact—

neck strong and supple, talons uncurled,
feathers soft, eyes gently closed.
Asleep like a human if not for the gaping cavity
that exposed his sternum to the sun.

I prayed this whitened calcium wouldn't snap,
pulled him from the sand,
laid him on the side of the bank.
My prayer was answered;

I covered him in dried needles
from the young pines all around,
and gave him the blessing
for any fallen creature:

Rest in peace, my friend.

And left him, wings slightly folded,
neck gently curled, face to the sky

Native To The Area

—Port Oneida, Michigan

Phillip Sterling

In autumn the sumac
primps as if for a first date

with a boy she's liked *forever*
her dress his favorite shade

of hunter green (according
to the sister in her grade)

and to be certain his attention
will be drawn to her best feature

just a smidgen of her mother's
dark red rouge

Dandelion Daydreams

Lauren Driscoll

You brewed me sumac tea and we munched on fried dandelions
The sun kissed the ground earlier than last
You spot gingers and cardamoms and berries in the trees
(Falls starts early this far north)
We snuck in one of the last swims of the season
The cold tickles my toes and freezes my femurs, the towel you warmed on your dashboard is a
cozy respite
And you, my refuge
We worship the glowing orange ball and cherish the chance for skin to dry with little effort
Heads rest on shoulders as jazz twirls the ends of my hair
Thoughts encircling western wildfires that provided this sultry sunset
I nod off as you drive me home, cabin in the woods with sapphic secrets and sour sumacs and
your favorite tee dancing in my laundry
I bid you adieu and close my eyes until sunrise
I lust for this life on cloudy days and starless nights
On days I want to lose myself in her arms instead of on trails

Strawflowers

Candace J. Lee

Pine needles skittering through fall
tangle into edging
now a basketful of garden
        stems nearly dislocate
        lean on coneflowers of Papaya
        and Marmalade—
                faded banners

                flag mums, spread apart their clusters
                        blossoms all bristled, a hint of perk
                        in a garden so tendered
                                so tousled by rabbits and rodents
                                flattened by my clompers
                                a tumbled old yucca and stray
                                        feather fanfare.

Light clouds today
maple leaf tumbles lose their blush
and coddle glaucous asters;
        though their lids lift as my shadow shifts
        this morning, I am wayward caught
        snagged by drooping seedheads—
                Dragon Blood sedum

                blanched overnight after mounding
                        dreams of Paprika, that boldest yarrow
                        now as anemic as the mallow.
                                Snakeroot bottlebrushes, arched
                                        into bottle-seed rattlers.
                                        Clusters of bee balm—
                                                bobbing dark omens.

Nose cold and dripping on cleome
phlox mildew has been climbing our legs
interwoven we remain
toes wiggling together
family roots, familiar soil.
Blink, and the last pollen drifts on
a shimmering memory.

Veronica left gray with split ends
musk of sandalwood smolders
as Blackeyed rudbeckia strives to outlast
mixed family huddles.
What petals remain—
a kiss of tissue tear-stains
shriveled buds.

Gusts whip up a drizzle then
Lake Michigan chills
busies the mites as geosmin
microshreds –
puts gardens to bed
family roots, familiar soil
turning into more

inward turning, all of us
ready to sacrifice
autumn's terrestrial show
to earthworms
when compost most lively
binned by sprigs and straw
a boon for the perennials among us.

Last Swim Of The Season

Susan Allen

A perfect day for popsicle feet
and knees and thighs, shoulders and skulls
We're game
You say "We'll dive under on the count of three"
One two three
You raise your hands above your head, pitch forward,
disappear
Within seconds you burst through the water,
Beating your chest, hollering
Then you notice
Me
— dry from my waist up
This is the only time I have ever cheated on you
My love

Bridge Of Seasons ©*Lisa Fosmo*

The Salmon Run

Russell Reece

Franny said she wouldn't be there when he got back. It had stopped him for a moment, the way she'd said it, how she'd locked her gaze with his and wouldn't break off.

"Up to you," he'd said, and walked out the door.

On the drive to the lake he'd replayed that conversation over and over. She was bluffing, he was sure of that, but he shouldn't have pretended not to care. He pulled on his chest-waders and carried his net and other fishing gear onto the beach.

Late October snow gusted off Lake Michigan as he pushed the stanchion into the sand and waded knee-deep to cast his bait. The rig flew through the snowy air and splashed far off shore. He tightened the line, felt the rhythmic pull from the rollers and set the rod in the stanchion. Dammit, he thought. He should be enjoying himself; finally out in the fresh air after working all week in that freaking office. Leave it to Franny to spoil the day before it began.

"I don't get it, Joey," she'd said. "Every weekend—what's so darn important about fishing?"

Why shouldn't he go fishing? He takes care of her, makes good money, they have a nice place. They do things together. She should cut him a break. But no, every weekend the same old shit. What's he supposed to do—go shopping or lie around the house, miss the salmon run?

He poured a steaming cup of coffee from his thermos, took a sip and watched the waves roll in. He shook off a chill. Overall, things were good. They got along. He loved her, couldn't imagine being with anyone else. If it wasn't for her nagging about fishing there would be no problems to speak of. And he was used to that now, had put up with it the entire four years of their marriage. She was worth the hassle. But today, for some reason, she took it over the edge. He stared out at the lake, his mind engulfed in a cloud of gloom.

A huge salmon leapt skyward in the vicinity of his bait. He grabbed the rod as it bent double, line playing out, the drag screaming. He slung the landing-net over his shoulder and waded in. This was a big fish; nothing to do now but hold on.

After nearly a minute, the salmon stopped. He tried to turn the fish, gain some line back, but it wouldn't budge. Then it started moving parallel to the beach and he was able to make a little headway. He would have to be patient, use all his skills. There would be no way to manhandle this fish.

He was in above his knees, the water crystal clear, the clean sandy bottom rippled from the movement of waves. Snow gusts were frequent and heavy. He was finally able to turn the fish and reel in line. He couldn't wait to see it. He thought of the fight with Franny but brushed it off.

Fifty feet away, the salmon swirled, its dorsal fin and broad tail breaking the surface. A monster, he thought. It made another short run then stopped and let him recover line. As he reeled, he backed up toward the beach, careful not to trip and fall in the chilly surf. He was in foot-deep water when the salmon glided into view—a Chinook, a big silver-sided female.

The powerful fish slowly circled him. A wrong move now and it could run, snap the line and be gone. He needed to pay attention. Snow gusted. Icy flakes peppered his face. After several tense minutes he led the fish into the net. It struggled for a moment then stilled, alive but fully spent.

He kept the net in the water and knelt alongside. It had to be 40 inches—the biggest salmon *he* had ever caught. Not a record but certainly big enough to spark attention. He imagined his picture with the fish on the wall at Ed's Sport Shop, celebratory beers at the tavern, maybe even an interview on the local TV station's outdoor show. Wouldn't Franny get a kick out of that? *I won't be here when you get back.*

His hand cradling the belly, he removed the hook from the fish's jaw. He was always taken by the colors—the dark purple head and galaxy of spots on the back and tail. This one was just as striking as all the others he had caught.

And then he saw Franny's determined glare again. There was something about it this time. What if she wasn't bluffing? The thought hit him like a shot. He went dead inside.

The salmon struggled. He stared at the fish for a moment, then pulled the netting away and freed it. It hovered in place, the swirling pectoral fins holding it upright.

"Go on," he said.

He thrashed the water with his hands. The fish began to move. "Go on. Get out!" he shouted. He got up and chased it, splashing through the shallows, over the rippled sand before falling face down on his hands and knees. Icy water soaked his clothes. Snow swirled madly around him.

"Damn you!" he said. "Damn you."

Some Evening Visitors

Paul Maxbauer

Coyotes call to one another,
yipping, barking, and howling.
They pause as if awaiting a reply,
then start up again.

Their cries resound across the valley
where I stand in a river and scan
for movement on a ridgeline
illuminated by the last narrow band
of yellow light, before darkness
descends.

The coyotes remain hidden, but I
count myself lucky just to be here,
to listen to the primordial chorus,
reminded of my status as a visitor
to this valley with an old, and still
unfolding geological history.

They move on and I hear quieter
sounds, the sighing of the alders
and poplars moved by a light breeze,
the swish of my casting, and the
music of water rushing past
rocks, boulders, and drowned trees.

I wade slowly, my eyes adjusting
to the deepening darkness,
hoping for one more rising trout to
try for, in no hurry to reach a landing.

Autumnal Equinox

Thomas F. Conlan

By the Escanaba River.

A glowing fire encapsulated by stones.
Coyotes howl at dusk.
Mister Jack Daniels and cherry juice
breathing wood smoke.
Two nibbles from a brook trout
hiding in a swirl
to avoid becoming dinner.

A place to come to terms
with haunting demons determined
to cast my thoughts astray.

A story on the battery operated radio,
a Menominee boy recalls his father.
Push harder, become the warrior.
Visit Spirit Rock, Grandfather warns,
you must focus,
for what you see first
will come to pass.

In the gentle morning, the river gurgles
while over the radio Bach
plays for many gods,
stills troubled waters.
Surely goodness shall follow me…

Rushing Waters (Canyon Falls) ©*Jennifer Uehlein Reynolds*

Whitetailing, Kehl Lake

Candace J. Lee

we arrive in boots
shivering among marsh doilies
        lacy, the crazed ice
lost if not for an Ojibwa marker-tree a
mong smokes of a lingering council circle
        our breath so misty
swirling the sheen free of a virgin lake

solitary and twenty feet out
a skater leans forward, leg raised
        until held arabesque
one arm floats back to grasp her blade
she lifts gaze, a hazy gazelle staring
        across ice at a figure
ghost-deer taut,
as she drifts closer he swivels
        one half revolution, snowy
white scarf slung down his back

we late arrivals are lacing up
hear her chuckle, her coos
        as she glides near him
lowers her arched limb
circles with a deep edge
        no question the man stiffens
then pivots
prongs, throwing up chips
        frost hangs undecided
flushed out by the settling sun

shouts from the western shore jar all
four of us flushed by the peach-rose
          metal hits ice, percussing forth
yells, scratches razor-crisp as couples
take shape under the jagged rims of firs
          and slice across shadows
spin out of dusk and race toward

us newlyweds at the edge
we try a revolution, make it halfway
          toes tingling in our skates
paw with the pick ridges
lean toward a stand of birch
          snow mitts land as we glance
in council, face each other

The Line ©*Grace Giroux*

Returning

Lisa Fosmo

I don't know why I stayed away so long.
Traveling now to the end of the good road,
to where old corduroy peeks out from dirt and rock.
Where someone once tried to build a road to god.

A gathering of boulders
memories of glacial descendants.
The sound of thirst quenching
Into its own throat.

The place Where eagles come
to watch their own shadows.

At night I sprawl across the dock
to watch the Northern lights inform the night sky,
as owls answer back across the lake.

In morning a loon is catching fish feeding her baby,
as it yips like a pup for more. The loon's song
so haunting echoes like a train whistle,
leaving me lonesome before I've even left.

The fork of an old two rut.
Green wild as fur dotted in daisies.
Pearls on parted emerald waves.
There I can almost see my old dog
waiting, tail wagging,

welcoming me back to my belonging.
And I only hear I love you from the ever
present ghost of loves past.

That Fall

Greg Rappleye

CATHLEEN (begins to keen): It's destroyed we are from this day. It's destroyed, surely.
—John Millington Synge, *Riders to the Sea* (1904)

We knew that salt cod is hideous,
fouled with *nematodes*, its gravy worse,
but had cartoons and were safe enough
for now, watching a frantic mouse drop anvils
on the head of a furious cat. We'd moved
north to Bob Eisele's, west of Marquette,
his swoopy red convertible angled out
along the Superior cliffs, its white canvas
top tied back against the lake wind, Old Bob
sipping bourbon, eating smoked chubs,
greasy fingers sorting the jumbled wires
of a classified gadget he'd cobbled up
in a fish house near the Soo.

A Western Electric crew followed him around,
burying Bob's secrets across the Keweenaw,
his wires wormed down deep, *To listen*
among the depths, was all Bob would say;
to catch a Kremlin voice, strayed across the arctic.
I can still hear her along those cliffs, singing
as the big men wrenched and welded and dug,
her blue sweater gathered about her ribs,
raucous terns wheeling and those saltless waves
heaving cold against the iron-gorged rocks,
her lyrics unknowable—some slurred,
some Irish, though Mam's songs
in those days were already *atonic*,
a word I'd know soon enough,
and sad beyond the other songs of earth.

A Happenstance

Thomas F. Conlan

Flash as high as my waist
not a deer.
Flash yellow before me
in the hours before dawn, in the fall
when Orion shines low in the western sky.

I had seen pictures the night before
of a nuzzle long and wicked,
knowing not the meaning of mercy.
Imagination plays tricks on a lone soul
in dark, deep woods.

A fern grows like a partridge
near the side of a dirt road.
A broken branch hangs awkwardly,
brings to mind a buck bent down to sniff,
yet sticks are not antlers.

Did I see a wolf that morning
or just menacing yellow eyes passing quickly?
An happenstance unmistakable, yet,
the sight of a wolf stays lodged in your being,
while you search for his wildness in your soul

The Guardrail

S.D. Dillon

Hauling logs with my dad, outside our house on the dunes,
Eastport, Michigan, top knuckle of your ring finger,
in the smoky quiet of venison, jerky, and trout,
the occasional woodpecker,
and trees: horses against the October sky.

I'm in jeans, boots, an Oxford sweatshirt.
Dad's in a new Carhartt that'll outlast the dunes, maybe the rocks.
A man walks over in a beard and flannel,
hat says Ralph's such-and-such Construction.
I'm Ralph, he says, doing the driveway next door
I can turn your roller coaster into a nice steady grade—
how'd you get that front wheel drive truck up here anyway?
That's not mine, I say, it's his—pointing to the fence guy.
I drive the sedan at the foot of the hill:
stick shift, great city mileage, but nearly lost it over the edge last winter.

Ralph nods, turns to my dad, says I'd raise it yea-high, widen it a bit.
I watch, wait for dad to chainsaw the logs—I don't know these things.
I'm just digging holes to bury three posts,
following behind the plow, happy not to veer from the drive.

Upper Peninsula Soundbites

Milton J. Bates

The ice honeycombs
and sinks in the lake, fizzing
like freshly poured Coke.

One peeper starts up.
Another chimes in. Soon all
are jingling their bells.

Soft tattoo of rain
on roof, then a metallic
tinkling in downspouts.

Loons channel the lake's
changing moods with mournful wail
and raucous laughter.

A grouse explodes from
aspen cover, desperate
to be somewhere else.

Sandstone caves resound
with double-bass whumps when storms
drive big lake swells in.

Rain freezes on trees,
turning branches to wind chimes
that click and rattle.

You can tell it's cold
when snow squeaks underfoot like
an old farmhouse floor.

Ice is booming on
the lake tonight,
a drumroll for the Northern Lights.

Black Stream, Scent Of Snow

CJ Giroux

I am drawn to dark, as I slog toward solstice,
to the span of the rail trail's asphalt river
circling the bulb garden, home to winter's dusk.

In June, this rich soil—its striped hostas aglow—
resembles a Greek god's eye, rimmed with kohl, but
I am drawn to dark, as I slog toward solstice.

I stare past the dried stems of aster, grapevine
to brown fields. I dream deer, stilled but then leaping,
circling the bulb garden, home to winter's dusk.

They resurrect pods of dolphins (sleek, grey as
petoskeys) orbiting what I don't see, for
I am drawn to dark. As I slog toward solstice,

these harts now shift into sighthounds—from a tale
I can't quite recall, decay (mixed with wonder)
circling a bulb garden, home to winter's dusk.

Beneath a clouded moon, hunters' shots echo.
Pulling my coat tighter, I lean into lack:
I am drawn to dark, as I slog toward solstice,
circle the bulb garden, head home to winter's dusk.

Emmet Escapades

Lauren Driscoll

I dream of you from time to time
Of soft pink lips and sunburnt thighs
Of Rustic Baker bread and sweet beet salad
Of sandy hikes and driftwood balance

You cut your hair, twelve inches gone
I've missed your string and brass based songs
I've missed your four leaf clover fun
We lost ourselves in the summer sun

It's winter now, our town is sleeping
You cross my mind while my cedar tea's steeping
While I forage for berries on the Bear River Trail
I picture your boot prints with every exhale

I dream of you from time to time
Of your favorite Short's beer with a twist of lime
Of sharing whitefish under shiny dead stars
Of slurpring fresh springs and laughing in dive bars

Of love that set with the Autumn solstice
Of Michigan memories that will never leave us

Harlow Creek ©*Milton J. Bates*

A Yooper Takes Shelter At Camp

Lisa Fosmo

The sticky fingers of the forest,
pat my head, comb my hair
as I pass under pine branches.
A makeshift path through a mix
of winter and spring where there
is no driving in close.

I become pack mule,
a pachyderm carrying cargo,
a gypsy with sacks of food,
gallons of water, bottles of magic
and cans of craft beer.

My love busy building a fire,
priming the water pump, chopping ice
blocking the outhouse door.
The outdoor shower a heave of ice and leaves.
I empty my boots, free the gems of winter
that catch as my feet sink snow to hip.

My afternoon perch a stepladder
on the the covered porch,
washing large windows
eyes to the lake still thick with ice.

The neighbors dog runs over for a visit
suckles and mouths my dangling bare foot
like a calf at an udder. She's an old friend
cries and whines not understanding this
new world and why we hadn't stopped by.
I find forgiveness in her generous brown eyes
with my offering of chicken scrapes.

At dusk one lone crane flies by
feathers in close more shadow than bird.
We watch the fire from the glass door
of the wood stove, flaming orange and quick
as a litter of fox kits.

The radio tuned to 103.3 Elmer Aho
bringing us comfort with old country
and folk music. His soft familiar Fozzy Bear voice
a Saturday evening Yooper Companion.

One last peek at an endless starry sky.
We nuzzle in bed.
The dark so large so peaceful it eats the world.
We came here to be small to disappear.
We drift off belonging now to the ever widening quiet,
waiting for the gift of morning.

Marianne's Handbag

Hailey French

On Tuesdays, Marianne went to the market. Standing on the subway platform, Marianne's back ached as the strap of her handbag dug into her right shoulder. When she was younger, she would carry around dainty purses that barely weighed a thing. With time, her handbag grew—much like the rest of her. People told her it wasn't good for her health to carry around such an enormous bag, but how was she supposed to get rid of anything?

She unlatched the gold clip of her handbag to the rush of Lake Superior wind catching her gray hair with a familiar hello. A family of four laughed near the tall grass that sprouted up from her hairbrush and ran around a crumpled up tissue. Marianne longed to jump right inside and join them. She could almost feel the cool lake water on her sore feet and pebbles getting caught between her toes, but she had to focus. She needed marinara for dinner tonight.

The market was calmer on Tuesdays, which was the way Marianne preferred. She never could get used to this restless city where people always seemed to be in a hurry even when they weren't. She scanned the aisles for the one garlic and herbs marinara that almost replicated her late husband's homemade sauce, a delicacy he always made on their anniversary.

"Your total is $4.32," the cashier said to Marianne.

Marianne thought that was a little steep for marinara, but she grabbed her wallet that lay in an open field of wild daisies. The wet-dirt perfume of nature made her feel like a small child. Realizing she was a few cents short, Marianne reached again into her bag and plucked three daisies from the ground and handed them to the cashier.

"That should cover the rest," Marianne said.

"Would you like your receipt?"

"No, that's alright."

Marianne's Handbag
©Hailey French and Anna Matzke

Marianne walked the hill to her brownstone which sat at the end of her block. She opened her handbag to a lovely Autumn day at the Sleeping Bear Dunes. Sand warmed her hand as she fished for her keys, finding them in the branches of an old birch tree.

The marinara bubbled when Marianne added in a few garlic cloves and a dash of cabernet. She placed two plates on the table and poured two glasses of wine. After she had finished boiling the pasta, Marianne sat down to eat.

"Happy anniversary," she said, raising her glass to the empty chair.

Opening her handbag, Marianne peered down to see her husband standing on the rocky shore of Lake Michigan. The moon lit up the world like it must have forgotten it was night, and the stars danced on the water. Her husband reached up and handed Marianne a petoskey stone, the same one he had given her the night they met. She placed the familiar stone to her heart and blew a kiss into the handbag towards him.

On Wednesdays, Marianne went to the library. Standing on the subway platform, her back ached as the strap of her handbag dug into her right shoulder. She didn't mind, though, because it held all the marvelous things she held dear—the sound of waves hitting the lakeshore, the smell of pines at dusk, her beloved.

Beer And A Bump

for Jim Enger
(2/26/1946–12/5/2013)

Art Curtis

Had beer and a bump
in honor of you, my friend.
Thoughts keep you alive.

Explored feeder streams
of Boardman near Kalkaska.
Spring fed? They were cold!

But the day was hot,
comparisons misleading.
Your thermometer

would have been useful.
Sixty four or less…Brookies!
We would have rigged up.

Afterwards, seated,
we'd have a beer and a bump.
Swap yarns, talk writing.

A Heathen's Beatitude

Emily Colby

Years of yellow augmented in my periphery
until my myopic eyes could no longer ignore.

This autumn used to be August, these oak leaves
were red before they fell and grew green again.

I never imagined a shade so citrus would suit me,
but I'll yield my red, my grey, to make room for this halcyon.

September's hearth glows
between rows of sunlight and sweet corn.

Beams knocking at the top of my head,
weaving into my scalp until brown hair shines golden.

I bend knobby knees into the ground,
and sunshine begs me to take root.

Yielding,
Dunes After A Winter Storm

Marsha Jane Orr

Sand yields.
Sometimes a lot of sand yields,
Fast in a winter storm,
Wind upon the flat field,
Pushed up dune against back door.

Sand yields to wind.
Sand yields to water.
Sand yields.
And yet holds itself in constant form,
Sand.
No wind nor water,
Turns sand to dirt or clay or myrrh.
Essential nature it remains land,
The changing unchangeable.
Still sand
Yields to what's present,
Without resistance,
Or unseemly rude glance,
Without glittering glamour or gore.
Sand yields,
And thereby
Never loses itself,
Sand.

Inextinguishable

Philip Rice

the rain came
just as they said,
it wasn't November yet

there was no moon—
"cancel everything," they said
but we didn't—

we sang anyway
the joy of summer
inextinguishable

All Through That Dark Season

Susan Allen

All through that dark season we hiked
Through spring, boots soaked in melted snow, barnacled with fresh mud
Through summer, gathering ticks on our legs
And bites and bumps from things hidden in the tall grasses
Through fall we kept on, until the deepening leaves were finally stilled
by snow
We exchanged hiking boots for snowshoes,
wore masks to shield from the cold,
Not the virus
Our names became laced together,
Our tracks made one
As you placed your foot down in the soft snow
Upon mine
One step at a time

Waiting On The Wind ©*Karen Walker*

Mulligan II

Christine Saari

For Kathy Davis

This year, for Thanksgiving, we are not driving South,
across the big bridge, toward the glitter of Detroit.
We are headed Northwest, into the woods.
We leave behind the city of Marquette,
the town of Ishpeming, homesteads, camps.

Finally, we reach the valley of the Mulligan,
the road narrow, snow-covered, rutted,
escarpments on the left, the right,
a small road through new growth pine.

We park the splattered truck,
wheelcart firewood, food supplies, water
on a winding path to our small log cabin,
a sauna once, now a camp retreat.

Years ago we wheeled in the cast iron stove,
the antique metal bed with its heart design,
gifts when Kathy and Bill Davis
emptied their camp in Grand Marais.
They will keep us warm and comfortable tonight.

The day is grey and gloomy, but suddenly
the setting sun sets the ridge on fire.
A golden glow lights up fir tree candles,
reaches distant woods, fades in waves.
Then darkness and cold descend.

Jon makes a fire, I light candles, kerosene lamps.
We move the table close to the stove,
play a game of scrabble, sip 51K and Guinness,
settle early into our sleeping bags, laid out on the bed.

Unaware that this Thanksgiving will be Kathy's last day on earth,
I drift into sleep, give thanks to our friends
for the warmth and comfort of this night,
think of tomorrow: We will eat a humble meal,
long for our loved ones, far away,
grateful to be alive.

Breathe December

John Lennon

Wind howled dunes,
And frost beaten shoreline
Harmonize below the open
Sky of an early sunset.
Breathe December in
Like the long night that it is.
Let it wash over you
Like honey as it clings
To your soul with promises
Of tomorrow,
Warming you for the winter
And leaving you open
For what the year ahead may bring.

Blue Ice (An Indirect Path) ©*Moon Seagren*

When Winter

Robert Vivian

Winter comes as evensong, as sore throat and runny nose and old sweater gathering fibers to itself to harvest a few more strings of warmth and winter comes as crisply creased page eager to be written upon and balled up piece of paper thrown to the floor after the umpteenth draft and creosote of blackened railroad track in the clack away miles ringing out in the distance so that listening itself is hallowed and winter comes as the hush inside a hush in the dark intimate space between breaths and the commencement of all shivering and trembling and other small body quakes of humility before the awesome power of zero weather, winter comes as handkerchief or tissue paper in every room on every table before the first teary sneeze, comes as moaning, sighing and sweeping of wind up in the naked branches knocking together in the steady percussion of a great forbearance one eyelash away from forgiveness, winter comes as the soft lights glowing around every curved body and surface so that everyone and everything is finally haloed and laid bare on the altar of the world with nothing left to hide or defend including our most helpless cries, winter comes as candle light truckling at the eye in Hopkins' poem and charcoal fires embering in the dark, afghans and broken shoe laces and cold starry nights where bells ring far away in their most pellucid chimes of forever, which reverberate even now down the hallways of our days, winter comes as steelhead in the rivers back from their oceanic voyage turning from chrome to the color of gravel and alders and dogwoods lining the banks like wild-haired women about to fling themselves into the sea not out of despair but sheer wildness and abandon, winter comes as cold fingers and hand warmers torn open with one's teeth so that the clear cellophane may be ripped off the face of this earth, winter comes as empty envelopes waiting to be filled with love letters and checks to monasteries, animal shelters, gas companies, and children's hospitals, beloved aunts and fevered pleadings to the dead, winter comes and winter swoons, winter bows down and winter towers high above in silent clouds aloft, winter comes carefully and holy of the great sudden peace in the deliverance of all nil, winter covers with ice and snow and the sacred hibernation of bears, winter sweeps and winter rolls out carpet after carpet after veil of blankness, winter makes the ice scraper a vital tool of survival and unfettered sight, winter does not speak but moans again, winter makes the old radiator clack with clunky warmth in the country school room, winter puts the still in stillness one snowflake at a time as carefully as a knitter's aging hands whose feeling is unmatched in the annals of human touch, winter inspires children to lie on their backs and make snow angels with great spontaneous joy that spans heaven and earth and the four directions, winter beckons and winter bends, winter shatters all records and winter moans again and winter somehow makes the sun more naked and the Pleiades brighter and also the moon and stars and the eyes of the ones we love, winter makes getting out of bed before dawn holier and more profound as if waking and rising is a cosmic journey we must learn again and again and again, winter comes in full bridal attire and the matrimony of the ear and the tongue and the first tuning of a cello feeling for F and G minor among the last taut strings waiting to be released in a joyful and sorrowful sob crying out in the darkness finally for every hurt to be healed.

Predator

Edd Tury

Canada's cold wind strips water
from Superior's surface
drives snow sideways
deep into the groaning forest

In the season of death I am alive
wind and snow scrape my face
cold air fills my lungs

It's here
time of dark skies
time of blood
time of the hunt

I slip into the big woods
take my place
among hungry predators
my animal awakens

I wait

vigilant

lethal

After A Vacation

Skip Renker

Just days ago, a warm wind
in the gap between peaks,
hawks finding a thermal,
oceanfront palm fronds
applauding their own dry wit,

but now the snow-filled spruce
again, monotonous cawing
of crows from upper limbs,
our home state above, around,
within, as if we'd never left—

we try to remember the skies
we played under, the answered
prayers, but work closes over us
like a thick manila envelope
sealed from above. Later,

though, we sit quietly,
bring our renewed attention
to ice crystals forming
at dusk, the beautiful skeletons
of the maple and the beech.

Winter Waltz

Joyce Brinkman

Branches holding snow
wearing evening gloves of white
invite me to dance

Wild Impatience

Philip Rice

The ice moved out
and the people came in,
that old tree on the shore
is still almost falling over.

Ships moved from harbor to harbor
waves went nowhere, and everywhere.

It was once said that humans
are symptoms of the universe,
serenely arriving—like a headache
or a gentle fever, almost unnoticed,
the result of millions of tiny unseen things
that led to that moment,
that end up nowhere at all in particular—

Nothing happened today.
Nothing at all. I waited.
I moved in and out
with measureless love, every motion
hoping for tomorrow,

with wild impatience,
for the next boat to come in.

At The Edge Of Magic

Edy Stoughton

There is a veil between the world and me
Muted, soft edges, gradations of gray
Cocooned and cozy inside I peer out as if through a gauze curtain
Outside the world is misty, muted, hushed
Blanketed in silence
Long rolling waves on the lake
Slow, heavy, relentless pounding on the shore
Chunks of ice on the curls
Like custard thickening on the stove.

The land is poised in anticipation
A stillness, a waiting
The only sound the lonely howling of the wind
We wait on the edge
Change is in the air
Through the white mist—transformation
Freezing happens on the mammoth lake at just this moment
Deep winter arrives on quiet wings
Magic happens in silence.

Periwinkle

Emily Colby

I find you in winter nights, playing peek-a-boo with the stars.
I find you in summer sunrise skies, my mom driving
beside me. We argue under your tease of retreating navy.

Do not envy my feet in the emerald grass of dewy spring.
I know the green of jealousy; I spent my childhood watching you
swirl and gleam and glimmer on Cinderella's midnight dress.

Yes, melancholy color of Lake Huron on a cloudy, autumn day.
Your waves dance on my cold skin like the Nutcracker's beloved
ballerina. Even your name suggests elegance as such.

You've made a home in the cataracted irises of wise old men.
As my father gets older, I see you creep into his eyes too.
I hope you might creep into mine.

I'm Thinking Of Us In A Cottage

Emily Colby

In the middle of a frozen forest,
waiting for mild June.
Ours are the only voices we've heard in months
besides the blue-white whistle of wind
through conifers, and the sorrowed howl
of a wolf runt we've named Max.

We pick wine-colored winter berries,
more sour than sweet, and I catch the thick hem
of my flannel dress on thorns in the brush.
Later I rest my legs in your lap, toes cold
no matter how many wool socks
you darn upon my feet. You weave a needle
into the ripped plaid of my skirts while I admire
how big your hands look
holding such a small, shiny thing.

We don't notice time passing
until one of us stops breathing.

In The Blue Hour

CJ Giroux

Snowdrifts divide, flow forward
to surround sinking structures.
White-water rapids tumble over, past boulders
both invisible and seen,
as streams of blue grow,
call our names, lead us onward.

The old barn is an emissary to the past.
Gaps grow between planks
the grey of driftwood in landlocked seas.
Winds move from whistle to scream—
the building groans, its spirit hole blocked.

Metal construction rises
over slumping hills, row after row
of gnarled trunks, arthritic branches.

Resembling aging protesters who lost the war,
old-growth cherry trees
bow beneath the rivering sky.
The horizon is split by steeples:
Baptist, Presbyterian, Catholic.
Shadows surround.

Footsteps link outbuildings in a tug of war.
Pools of snowmelt follow
the weight of man,
become nothingness.
Granary, garage, shed, lean-to
lean from, shed the old ways.
The sky, ground grow blue.

Djinn Of The Bay ©*Tamar Charney*

Silencing The Refrain

Tamar Charney

Julia walked down the stairs to the beach and was smacked by the wind. It was fifteen degrees. Snow stung her. She'd forgotten the cold blowing in off Lake Michigan hurt.

She'd spent the morning trying to practice, but just couldn't bring herself to play more than a few bars at a time. Instead of losing herself in her music and her work, she kept feeling her body tense up as images of Kevin's death flooded her mind. She hadn't watched the video ISIS posted of his execution; the visions in her mind were bad enough.

Julia had known Kevin's job was dangerous, but she didn't pay a lot of attention to international news. When he was off somewhere on assignment, she'd sometimes pull up his reports online, but that was primarily to see his face, hear his voice, and have some sense of the part of the world he was in. All she hears now when a TV is on, or anyone speaks to her, is a repetitive dirge like larghissimo passage that gets stuck in her head for hours. *Kevin is dead. Kevin is dead. Kevin is dead.*

She retreated to the only place where the refrain is silenced, the beach.

Usually, she could stand here for a long time being blown by the wind, watching the waves roll in, but today she wasn't sure how long she'd last. Tears welled in her eyes, not from sadness or grief, but from the wind. It felt good to cry and not hurt emotionally. Each day for the past week she stood here. The wind and waves might blow it all away, she told herself. The roar and physical force of wind did leave her with nothing but quiet in her head. She wished she could stay longer, but her face had gone numb.

She turned and noticed the sand and snow had the fudge ripple ice cream effect she hadn't seen in years. The white snow and the brown sand formed perfect swirls. As a kid she'd thought if she scooped it up with an ice cream scoop, it would taste sweet and melt in her mouth instead of being gritty and gross.

She realized she smiled at that memory. Her face hadn't assumed that shape in weeks.

Maybe her mom had been right to send her the plane ticket home for Christmas, even though Julia didn't really think of Petoskey as home anymore. Julia had almost refused. Her mom probably couldn't afford it. Making a living in northern Michigan was hard. Her mom had sacrificed a lot to send her to the music school, even with the scholarships. But Julia knew the ticket was her mom's way of trying to help. And her mom was right—staying in Kevin's condo without Kevin during the holidays was a recipe for despair.

Normally, it was Julia who sent her mom a plane ticket to come to California to escape the long, dark Michigan winter. Julia couldn't even remember when she was last in Petoskey. The cold seemed so much worse after so many years in LA, though everyone said how much warmer it was these days. She hardly recognized the place, it was more chichi than she remembered. All the Chicago and Bloomfield Hills women with their yeti boots and plastic surgery. It seemed like LA was spreading.

It took two seconds to pick out the locals from the big city women. It wasn't just the fashion. The locals were weathered, their hands large from work. It was odd to see women her mom's age working at cash registers, serving food, and doing the jobs the teenagers did back in LA.

Life was hard up here. Sure, the shores were lined with multimillion-dollar homes and the bays dotted with expensive yachts in the summer. But those people mostly came up here for summers and weekends. They bought expensive clothes at the little boutiques in Petoskey and ordered top-shelf drinks at dinner. They kept the economy going. Sort of.

Many of Julia's childhood friends were still here waiting tables, cleaning hotel rooms, or if they'd gotten lucky, teaching. It would have been so easy to have been one of them and still be here.

She'd be getting heavy, her naturally blond hair graying rather than dyed black, and while she'd surely have had the kids she'd wanted to have with Kevin, she'd also have been divorced at least once by now. It's how things worked. That nice boy would end up hitting the bottle too hard after losing a job, perhaps fall into cooking meth or just doing something stupid to turn a buck that put the kids at risk. She heard too many of the stories about her former classmates from her mom.

Because of music, she had escaped this place, first in spirit, then in body. The music she studied as a kid taught her about people and places beyond northern Michigan. Then it became her ticket out. Now it was as though she'd never been a part of this place.

After dinner with her mom, she drove a few miles up the road to try to sneak into the hot pool at the condos. She'd heard about it from an older guy she'd dated one summer in high school. He cleaned the pool there and told her that in the summer someone checked cars at the entry gate, but in the winter you could just drive in. Over the holidays and on some winter weekends, when the summer people came up to celebrate or ski, the outdoor swimming pool was turned into a giant hot tub.

She learned from performing that you could walk in anywhere if you looked the part and acted as if you belonged. She could walk into any theater or concert hall before a show and not be stopped—even when her cello was already there. Other people would get stopped, but of course she was meant to be there, and somehow others knew.

She didn't dare try things like that as a teenager, she knew her place growing up, she wasn't one of them. But Julia knew she kind of was one of them now. She didn't look like a local anymore. She didn't quite look like a summer person either, but perhaps she could pass as a hipster relative. She just pretended she was coming from one of the units in the back and slowly walked into the dressing room, stripped down to her bathing suit, and went out into the hot pool.

It was empty, the water perfectly still, and it glowed with that otherworldly green created only by underwater lights in a swimming pool. Completely artificial but oddly pleasing.

Snow was falling. And then not falling. The moon shining and then not shining as bands of lake-effect snow shimmied overhead. She floated in this silent netherworld. Where did she belong? Not here, not there, kind of nowhere. Kevin had been an anchor for her, and now all that was left was the music that recently seemed to be drifting away from her.

She floated on the surface of the warm water while snowflakes melted into her eyebrows. She relaxed for the first time in weeks and then immediately tensed wondering if she could trust the feeling. Every time she'd thought she was beyond the oppressive phase of grief, it would descend on her again, it's darkness and intensity reminding her of the storms that would come in from Lake Michigan every November when she was a child. Dark grey clouds would suddenly arrive, moments later the driving wind and soaking rain would begin and could last for minutes or days. Her emotions felt about as unpredictable as those fall storms off the lake.

But when Julia got back to her mom's she dragged a crate of her old scores out from under the bed and began to play works she hadn't performed since Kevin had come into her life.

Woods Walk ©*Elizabeth J. Bates*

19th Annual Crooked Tree Arts Center Juried Young Writers Exposition

Walloon Writers Review is delighted to share the poetry and prose winners for the 2021 19th Annual Crooked Tree Arts Center Juried Young Writers Exposition. This event is a collaboration between Crooked Tree Arts Center, Petoskey News-Review, the Bob Schultze Fund for Creative Writing at the Petoskey-Harbor Springs Area Community Foundation, Little Traverse Literary Guild, McLean & Eakin Booksellers of Petoskey and Walloon Writers Review.

Hanna-Renkes/Jan Smith Literary Award

Best In Show Poetry

Introduction to Womanhood

Grace Daniel
Grade: 11, Petoskey High School

Puberty, getting groomed, and being seen as only phases
Don't they see how easy they have it?
They have it better than most will admit
They don't have built in survival kits
They don't see the lens they have been accustomed to
The patriarchy clings to them and their perspectives are askew
A true mother knows when their sons are doomed
When the propaganda in the media about women is consumed
Doubled up victims and the porn industry
We consume it like it's not bigotry
I've been followed one too many times to not be afraid
Tired of this ongoing manic pixie dream girl charade
It's an awakening to a nightmare and realizing it's your reality
That all you're viewed as is your sexuality
It's not all men but it's most
My femininity wants to hide like a scared ghost

Vaccine Verse

Carley Sneddon
Grade 12, Petoskey High School

The expressed objective; protection for the collective
Immunity in our community, and a cultivated unity
Ours is reliance on the study of science
Which urges compliance through evidence and guidance

Please continue to honor those we've lost
And the front-line workers that bore the cost
Who promised to protect and honored their oath
Even as illness saw exponential growth
Please rise to the occasion, and get your vaccination

Respect the scientists and biologists, the epidemiologists
The PHDs in biochemistry
Clinicians, statisticians, diagnosticians and physicians
Who've battled opposition to eradicate this condition
Help them achieve their mission and stop the transmission

Celebrate those in immunology and the study of virology
Their research converging to stop the surging
A path of dedication led us to this destination
mRNA will lead the way for all of us to be okay

Please sign up for your shot today

A network of benefit to which you extend
Directly to your neighbors, your elders, and friends
Our grocers, drivers, and mail carriers too
All of those who've kept working and will continue to do

We're all connected; so please don't go unprotected
Others will be subjected to the effects of even one who's reckless
If there's trepidation, speak to your doctor for an explanation
We need to stop the contagion, and do our part for containment

Soon we will all stand together in celebration
Our minds and bodies filled with elation
Of the time we thought of other's lives
So that no one else would have to die
And with this, a final declaration and supplication
To safeguard yourself, your friends and relations
Please abide by your obligation
And sign up today to receive your vaccination

Passing Notes

Isabel Dunn
Grade:10, Great Lakes Learning Academy (Virtual)

The first day of school was not James Murray's favorite time of year. There had been a time when he enjoyed it. Once, he had actually been excited. He had just gotten a new haircut, and he was looking forward to showing it off. But when he heard some kids snickering behind his back, the words 'ugly' and 'stupid' coming out of their mouths, his day had been ruined.

Now that he was a junior, he wasn't worried about seeing his classmates again, but he couldn't say that he was excited. He kept his head down and stayed quiet. That was how he had learned to get through it all.

His first class of the day was history. When he entered the classroom, he noticed a girl that he had never seen before sitting at a desk in the back. He wondered who she was.

James learned her name when attendance was taken. The teacher called out, "Camila Pérez?" and the girl raised her hand. He couldn't help but notice the subtle cringe she gave at the pronunciation of her name.

"You can call me Millie," she said.

"Alright, Millie," the teacher replied. "I don't think we've met. Where are you from?"

"Puerto Rico. I moved here with my family over the summer."

"That's wonderful. I hope we can make you feel at home."

Millie smiled slightly and nodded. "Thank you."

After class, James saw a group of boys approach Millie in the hallway.

"Hey," one of them said, "You're from Puerto Rico, right? Can you speak Spanish?"

Millie nodded.

"That's cool! I can speak Spanish too!" he grinned. "My-o name-o is-o Elias-o." Then, with a chuckle, he added, "Uno, dos, tres, taco!"

Millie rolled her eyes. "Eres un estupido," she muttered, walking away. James was impressed. He didn't speak much Spanish himself, but he had a pretty good idea of what Millie had said. He admired her bravery. He knew he never would have been able to do something like that.

In English that day, James was pleased to see that Millie was in the same class that he was. He smiled and introduced himself, but didn't do much talking beyond that. They didn't get to know each other until a week later when the note-passing began.

Before long, James realized that English was not his favorite class. Each day, the students received a worksheet that took ten minutes to complete. However, the teacher didn't start the lecture until thirty minutes had gone by, so there was a good twenty minutes at the beginning of class where nothing was happening. The teacher had strictly forbidden talking, so James had taken to reading a book. That was until he felt a slight nudge against his arm.

James glanced over and saw that Millie was sliding a notebook to him. At the top of the page, she had written, *Even I could teach English better than this guy.*

James laughed and pulled out a pencil. *I'm sure you could,* he replied.

Millie smiled and scribbled, *Is that a good book you're reading? Sorry for interrupting you.*

No, it's okay, James wrote back. He paused for a moment, then added, *I've been meaning to tell you: what you did on the first day of school was pretty cool. With Elias, I mean.*

Thanks. Did you understand what I said?

No, but I think I got the message.

Glad to hear it. I may have been overreacting, but I can't stand it when people mock Spanish by adding the letter o onto the end of a word. Spanish is such a beautiful and complex language, and I hate seeing it reduced to a joke like that.

I don't think you were overreacting, James replied. *You probably face a lot of that around here, right?*

People can be ignorant, she admitted. *It's what I expected, though. Being the new kid is never easy, and being the new kid from a different country…you know how it is.*

"Mr. Murray, what are you doing?" James looked up from the notebook to see the teacher glaring at him from his desk. He cleared his throat and held up his pencil.

"Just taking notes," he said. Satisfied with that answer, the teacher went back to his lecture. James glanced over at Millie, and they both smiled. English had just gotten a whole lot better.

Over the next few weeks, James and Millie continued to pass notes. James learned that Millie was really good at telling jokes, but she was also nice to talk to about serious things. The more that he talked to her, the more he began to like her.

Around Halloween, the homecoming dance was advertised across the school. People were getting dates left and right, and James decided that he wanted to ask Millie out. He knew that it was a simple question, and that, even if she said no, she would be nice about it, but he wanted to do it the right way. Finally, he decided what that way would be.

In English, after a few minutes of passing the notebook back and forth, James gathered up all of his courage and wrote, *Millie, there's something I want to ask you.*

Ask away, she replied.

James took a deep breath, then wrote, *¿Quieres ir al baile conmigo?*

Millie read over his note, then looked up at him with a big smile. *"Sí,"* she replied. "Yes, of course I do."

"Miss Pérez," the teacher snapped, drawing everyone's attention to James and Millie. "No talking."

"Sorry," Millie said, but the smile hadn't left her face. She looked over at James and reached under her desk to brush his hand. James took it in his and smiled back. In that moment, he *couldn't* have been happier.

Bob Schulze Award for Prose – High School

First Place

Ghost Stories

Bella Lennon

Grade 9, Charlevoix Montessori Academy of the Arts

Ashley was having an average day before she walked straight into a ghost. Everything was going normally. Her little brother woke her up by being a menace, her mom yelled at her to get up several times before she actually stumbled out of bed, and she rushed, tripping several times on her way to the bus. Everything was playing out just like it always did. School was boring and she was supposed to pay attention, but instead, she built eraser towers and passed notes to her friends. The only captivating classes were choir and PE. She had a great time running around in PE and singing in choir. Everyone thought she was trying to be a showoff, but in all honesty, she was just trying to have fun. It's not like she cared what they thought anyway.

Soon school was over, and it was time for her to go take care of the cemetery. She started taking care of the cemetery when she was 11. She thought that it would make the place look a little bit nicer and would respect those who have passed. She swept through all the graves, pulled out the surrounding weeds, and sang songs while working. She was also not the only one who had been taking care of the cemetery. There was this guy who always came to place flowers on the graves. She usually just missed him or got there when he was just about to leave. She tried to talk to him a couple times before, but he never answered her. He always looked nervous when she managed to catch him, but she didn't know why. He looked about her age and she had seen him a couple times in the town and in her school, but they never actually talked.

Today, as autumn was right around the corner, leaves had fallen scattering on top of graves in the cemetery. Looking through the gate, she admired how beautiful it looked. In horror stories and scary movies cemeteries are always depicted as spooky and creepy, but on this nice cool morning with the sun shining and the sky as blue as ever, the cemetery looked anything but scary. It always had a magical feel, like it was separate from the rest of the world. Today as she arrived, she noticed the guy had just arrived too with a big bouquet of flowers. This was pretty unusual for him, but she said nothing about it. He came up and opened the gate, and they both walked in together. They both walked in, through a ghost.

For the first time in his life, after Eli walked through that ghost, his mind was completely blank. Which was pretty weird considering his mind was never blank. He always had a continuous inner dialog that never stopped. This made sense because it's not exactly like he could voice his thoughts out loud, he was mute. He was born with vocal cord paralysis, which is a condition that causes one vocal cord to not be able to reach the other, and this leaves a gap between the vocal cords. When he was born he was perfectly healthy otherwise, so his parents decided not to undergo treatment and assumed his voice would get better with time. It was quite the opposite. Over time, his voice got weaker and weaker until at 3 years old he could no longer talk. His parents asked if he could get surgery so he could speak again. The doctors explained it would be dangerous because it could damage his vocal cords even further. So his parents had to adjust to having a mute son, and their son had to adjust to being mute.

Which brings us to today. Where, for the first time in Eli's life, his mind was completely blank, while walking through a ghost. School was fine. Eli did what he usually did. He stayed in the back, and didn't attract any attention to himself. You see, Eli wasn't exactly "popular" among all the high-schoolers at his school. People thought he was weird for not being able to talk. They usually avoided him, and when they had to talk to him, they would talk like they couldn't understand him or like he was 5. Eli didn't mind the whole "kids his age not talking to him" part. He found it hard to socialise anyway. Whenever he had to communicate with someone, he would use the white board he carried around everywhere to communicate. He would write down what he wanted to say and then show it to the person he was talking to. It was a simple yet slightly annoying process because writing down absolutely everything takes time.

After school he quickly gathered his things, and hurried to get to his Grandma's flower shop and the cemetery. Luckily his Grandma's flower shop wasn't too far from where he was. He picked up a bouquet of flowers as fast as possible and booked it to the cemetery. When he got to the cemetery, the girl was already there. Usually he managed to get there before she did, or sometimes after. Today, there she was, just standing there looking through the gate. This girl often came to the cemetery to clean it up and make it look nice. He'd also heard her singing there a couple of times. They'd never actually had a conversation together, even though they've both been taking care of the cemetery for about 2 years. He always tried to either get there before or after she did, or try his best to get out of there quickly when she was around. He didn't want to be rude by ignoring her or anything, it was just easier to avoid confrontation. Before he lost his nerve, Eli walked up to the gate and opened it. The girl gave him a funny look but didn't say anything. They then both walked in together. They both walked in, through a ghost.

Dear Society

Riley Cannon
Grade 7, East Jordan Middle School

Society today
Is worse than yesterday
Especially for the girls
Always getting judged

You tell us to not wear makeup
Yet judge every little detail
But if we wear a little more
You tell us that we are trying too hard

You tell us to dress comfortable
Yet say "It's not pajama day," and run away
But if we dress a little nicer
You tell us that we are trying too hard

You assume that we are indestructible
Like we can't be hurt
And the second we start to cry
We are suddenly a little baby

If we don't get good grades
You call us dumb
Yet if we do get good grades
We are suddenly a nerd

When will we not be pressured?
Will it ever end?
"She's not pretty"
"She can't sing"
"She's a nerd"
EVERYONE STOP!

I yell
I get angry
No more reputation
Will it ever end?

I am more than that
We are more than that
Girls are strong

No matter what
Even if you play with our emotions
Give us a break

Dear Society,
Will it ever end?

Bob Schulze Award for Prose – Middle School

First Place

George

Luke Washington
Grade 8, Petoskey Middle School (Remote Learning)

The experiment was first tested on George. The disease had slowly crippled him over the course of just three months and his condition would only get worse. His handlers were dejected. George had worked his way into their hearts with his quirky personality and mischievous antics. But, during the last month, they watched in despair as the simplest tasks like picking up a ball became impossible for him to perform. He was afflicted with a debilitating disease that also affects humans: amyotrophic lateral sclerosis or ALS.

Doctor Anthony Smith had been observing George's condition from the start. Last night, he was up most of the night, his face pressed to the eyepiece of his microscope, so that he was surprised he hadn't left a permanent mark on his face. Today, he was exhausted, but he arrived at the lab early anyway. His clothes were rumpled, but he didn't care. It was a big day for him and an even bigger day for George. He couldn't afford to waste any time.

He opened the door to George's room and made his way to his desk. Some of his colleagues were already in the room observing the diseased chimp and looked expectantly in his direction. He knew what they were thinking. Had he uncovered anything that would help George? Had he received the necessary approval?

Picking up his data sheet, Doctor Smith made his way over to where George was resting. The others looked sadly on. After a quick inspection of George, it was clear that the poor chimp didn't have much time left. The data showed that there had been another large decrease in George's active nerve cells. Luck was on George's side though. That morning, Doctor Smith had received the green light for the procedure. He gave his coworkers a nod and said, "It's time."

The procedure began at 11:00 a.m. Doctor Smith took a deep breath to calm his nerves. He felt as though he were standing on the edge of a cliff. So much depended on the outcome of this operation. It involved a new technology, not approved for humans, which if successful, could be used on them in the future. To the doctors, it made perfect sense to attempt the operation on George. Without the operation, George would die. Doctor Smith went over to the chimp to try to comfort him as the other doctors put him under anesthesia.

At 2:33 p.m., the procedure was over. The doctors and nurses stood quietly around him, some recording his vitals, others monitoring his appearance, and still others just wanting to be near to comfort him when he woke up. The magnitude of what they had done hung in the air. For the first time, the doctors had successfully inserted a large amount of small computer chips into an animal. If the operation was successful, the chips would serve as a replacement for the dead nerve cells caused by ALS. This could allow George to control his limbs again.

At 3:14 p.m, George began to stir. He awoke with a dazed expression on his face. Slowly, his eyes moved around the room and he seemed to recognize the eyes that stared back down at him. As the minutes passed, it was soon clear that the first step of the experiment had been successful. George had survived the surgery. Now, there was just one question left: did the surgery fix his disease?

Dr. Smith quickly retrieved a bag from a cooler in the corner of the room. George's eyes followed his movements as he reached inside the bag and pulled out a bunch of colorful fruits. They were George's favorites: strawberries and blackberries. Dr. Smith set them on the table in front of George. George's gaze fixated on the fruit; it was obvious that he wanted them. In his current state, however, it was impossible for him to grab a fruit. This could all change, however. Right beside the fruit lay a single button. When pressed, the button would activate the computer chips inside of George.

The other doctors in the room stared nervously at Dr. Smith, waiting. He reached a trembling hand towards the button. The instant the button was pressed they would know whether all of their research and hard work had paid off. As Dr. Smith pressed the button, the room grew deafeningly silent. George remained perfectly still, his eyes focused on the fruit. And then...

George lifted his arm, grabbed a berry, and ate.

Fairies' Night Dance

Grace Sullivan
Grade 5, St. Francis Xavier

Out in the deep dark sky
The specks of silver and gold.
With the bright, full moon that shimmers
And the owls, strong and old.
The shadows of the trees
Dance in the twilight.
Glistening rays that stream
Blowing on one perfect night.
Out in the constellations light flows
Casting down on the ground.
Illuminating under the sky,
What no one has yet found.
A fairy dance, out in the dark
The moon as their spotlight.
Violet costumes that shine like sparks
Their wings are so delicate and white.
They have technique so extravagant
They do their pirouettes.
The air so quiet and pure
Their crescent silhouette.
As they do their tricks and turns
They see the yellow sun.
They fly back to their household
And there the dance is done.

Life As I Knew It

Julie Retherford
Grade 5, Petoskey Montessori

Starting Here
Okay, here we go.
Yes, I'm 11
Yes, I'm in 5th grade
Yes, I have an Edge
It's part of me.
You don't know what the Edge is?!
Haha, well picture this:
A large segment of nothingness.
Darkness,
A Blank.
Picture a large gust of wind,
Or a tidal wave,
Shoving you into the nothingness.
Picture the only way getting out,
Is through a rope and harness,
Which someone else has to hold.
Who knows how long you'll be down there?
And No, you can not get out yourself
The Edge
It traps your screams.
It takes your breath.
It tells you
"No, you can't"
"You're hopeless"
"You're just not good enough"
"Don't try calling for help"
You're stuck down there.

Until someone hopes,
Until someone sees the rope,
And either,
Up you go,
Or down you go,
Deeper.
Trust
Who can I trust?
In this world full of people?
Who will hold the rope?
Friends?
Family?
Who will watch you fall?
Down
Down
Deeper.
I'm unsure myself.
Stuck
Hearing the voices,
In my head.
"Over there!" The Edge demands.
I am thrown into my own closet,
The tears welling in my eyes.
"Look at you," The Edge coos. "So...Helpless."
"Let me OUT!" I bang on the door.
The Edge laughs.
And I'm still in the closet,
Alone.
Hope?
I feel a tug at my chest.
Someone has grabbed the rope.
"Huh?" Calls the Edge.
I'm going up.
Higher,
And faster.

"Leave her down," growls the Edge.
Whoever is pulling the rope slips.
But I don't fall.
I keep going up.
"DOWN!" Barks the Edge
But whoever is pulling the rope is determined.
Very determined.
And up I go.
Racing to the top,
And before I know it,
I've reached it.
The Unknown Figure
I land in front of a girl,
About my age,
Who's a bit taller than me.
She's shaded by the darkness.
The Edge is not happy.
I start sliding back down.
The girl reaches out her hand,
And I grab it.
"NOOO!" Cries the Edge.
The girl helps me up.
But the Edge knocks us back again
"YOU," The Edge says.
I know it's talking to me.
"YOU HAVE NEVER DESERVED TO NOT BE WITH ME,"
The girl stands up.
She balls her hands into fists.
Something's coming.
The Unknown Figure VS The Edge
The Edge looks at the girl.
There is a moment of silence.
And then,
"YOU," The Edge is now talking to the girl.
She doesn't quiver.

She doesn't shake.
She doesn't even move.
"YOU DO NOT DESERVE TO LEAD THE GIRL!!" The Edge booms.
"Well then neither do you."
I gasp.
"She deserves to be happy, just as much as anyone else."
And she keeps going.
The Unknown Figure's Speech
"Always being down with you is NOT something she wants,"
She looks at me.
"And I know."
The Edge is silent.
"Do I deserve to be happy?"
I ask her.
"YES!!" She says.
She grabs my hands and helps me up.
"I don't know who you are,"
I whisper.
"But thank you."
And before I know what I'm doing,
I hug the girl.
And she gives me the biggest hug back.
"You deserve to live the happy life that is planned for you,"
The girl says in my ear.
"Without the Edge"
I'm Back
I look around me.
Everything looks like it is getting played in slow motion.
The Edge is melting.
Melting.
The girl exits the hug,
And vanishes
The Edge screams its last goodbye.
And that's the last time I hear the Edge.
I shut my eyes.

And when I open them,
I'm back.
In my bedroom,
Outside of my closet,
With Mona,
In my bed.
Mona lifts her head.
She knows.
Seeing the Girl
"Come on, do it!"
My brother shouts up the sledding hill.
He has created,
A double-jump.
I grip my sled.
Should I? I ask myself
"Yes," replies a voice.
I spin around.
"Huh?" I say.
"Up here," says the voice.
I look up.
Sitting on a tree branch,
Swinging her legs,
Still shaded by the darkness,
Is the girl's silhouette.
"You should," she says.
And when she says it,
I want to do it.
The Girl, Unshaded
I'm sitting in my room,
Reading.
Flipping the pages,
Until,
"Psst!"
I look up from my book.
And there stands the girl.

But I can see her face.
And she's beautiful.
She got stunning blue eyes,
Long dark brown hair,
A lovely smile,
She's wearing a dark blue sweatshirt,
And some black leggings,
And a dark blue hat to match her sweatshirt.
I gasp.
"You're the girl that helped me beat the Edge!"
"Of course."
Meeting a New Friend
I shut my book,
Hop out of my bed,
And invade her with a hug.
And she hugs me back.
I pull away,
Grab her hand,
And invite her up onto the bed.
She hops up,
And so do I.
"Thank you for helping me," I say.
"Anytime," The girl says quietly.
"So, what should I call you?"
"I have a name,"
"Really? What is it?"
The girl smiles.
"After all this time-"
She smiles more.
"You've finally found me. I'm Confidence."
My Inner Confidence
"Confidence,"
I breathe.
I like that.
Then something clicks.

But Confidence says it before me.
"I've been inside your heart, trying to show myself,"
Confidence pauses.
"And now I'm here. And my purpose is to help you."
I smile at her.
"And you already have."
And my heart glows,
And it feels as if,
Confidence is sending good thoughts into my brain.
And now when I need her,
She's there.
A New Start
It's a Saturday,
Mona is laying on her bed,
Chewing a deer antler,
My Grandpa gave to her.
Confidence smiles at me.
And I smile back.
I close my eyes,
And think about where I am.
Finally centered, I'm starting over, without the Edge.
I have a new friend, Confidence,
And I'm here.
And happy.
Happy to be me.

Contributors

Susan Allen: A lifelong poet and summer resident of Northern Michigan, Sue Allen has authored two books based on Mackinac Island. Her fiction novel *Water Beyond the Bridge,* is a later-in-life love story. Her non-fiction work, *Lilacs, A Fortnight of Fragrance on Mackinac Island,* was published in 2020. A former teacher in Fairfax County, Virginia, Sue continues to help other writers with editing, proofreading and inspiration.

Michele Austin was raised in Northern Wisconsin by native Yoopers. To her, the Upper Peninsula is synonymous with happy because her grandparents and great-grandparents all resided there, along with several other extended family with frequent visits to Ishpeming, Palmer, Negaunee and Marquette. Michele is a travel photographer. She is a published poet and essayist, Ultimate Killer Sudoku addict, avid ballroom dancer and in a band. She is easily distracted from worthwhile projects by the call of karaoke.

Elizabeth J. Bates lives in the Upper Peninsula, which provides ample opportunity for photography. Her photos have graced the covers of three publications, Richard Rastall's Anthology, *Maiden Voyage*, Milton Bate's collection of poems, *Stand Still in the Light* and edition 6 of *Walloon Writers Review,* as well as placing in local photo contests and exhibits.

Milton J. Bates is the author of books about Wallace Stevens, the Vietnam War, and the Bark River watershed in Wisconsin. His poetry includes the collection *Stand Still in the Light* (2019) and two poetry chapbooks, *Always on Fire* (2016) and *As They Were* (2018). He lives in Marquette, Michigan.

Joyce Brinkman, Indiana Poet Laureate 2002-2008, believes in poetry as public art. She creates public poetry projects involving her poetry and the poetry of others. Her own poetry is on permanent display in a twenty-five-foot stained glass window in an airport, in lighted glass artwork at a library, and on a wall in the town square of Quezaltepeque, El Salvador. A founding board member of the not-for-profit Brick Street Poetry Inc. Joyce has received fellowships from the Mary Anderson Center for the Arts, the Vermont Studio, and the Indianapolis Arts Council. Joyce has relatives in Michigan and loves visiting, particularly the Upper Peninsula. She is a graduate of Hanover College and lives in Zionsville, Indiana, with a cantankerous cat.

Tamar Charney is a writer, journalist, and photographer based in Ann Arbor who hides out near Petoskey. She's currently a Consulting Senior Supervising Producer for National Public Radio (NPR's) cinematically produced history podcast *Throughline*. Her name may be familiar to many public radio listeners in Michigan from her years of work at Michigan Radio. Tamar's photography and creative writing have been published by *Michigan Quarterly Review, Midwestern Gothic, Public Radio International,* and other outlets.

Emily Colby is, first and foremost, a cat mom. She is also a recent graduate of Central Michigan University's Creative Writing Program. In her time not spent at her job as a barista, Emily can be found taking pictures of sunsets, reading chunky fantasy novels, and shopping second-hand. She is learning to consider herself "a real writer," and hopes to eventually publish many books.

Thomas Ford Conlan, author of the lyrical memoir, *My Journey Begins Where the Road Ends,* has published poetry and prose in literary journals around the USA. Look for his novel, *Gentle Spirits*, to be published in the coming year. His collection of poetry and visual art, *Secret Conversations*, should follow shortly thereafter.

Art Curtis had written thousands of words of advertising and commercial copy when he turned to poetry in 1991 after reading Jim Harrison's, *Letters to Yesenin* during a major personal crisis. Perhaps it's his years of writing for radio that influences his belief that poetry is an oral/aural art form in which poet and listener form a perfect feedback loop, a theory that has been profoundly tested by COVID. Art read for several years with the Central Michigan

Poetry Quartet and up until March of 2020 read episodically at other venues.

Jim Daniels' *Gun/Shy,* published by Wayne State University Press, is Jim Daniels' eighteenth poetry book. Other recent books include his sixth fiction collection, *The Perp Walk,* and his anthology, *RESPECT: The Poetry of Detroit Music,* co-edited with M. L. Liebler, which was a Michigan Notable Book and received the Tillie Olsen Prize from the Working-Class Studies Association (both published by Michigan State University Press). A native of Detroit, he lives in Pittsburgh and teaches in the Alma College low-residency MFA program.

Bonnie Dankert grew up exploring the lake country surrounding the family's summer cottage in northern Michigan. A former high school teacher in Santa Cruz, California, for thirty-four years, Bonnie taught American Literature with a focus on the natural environment including wilderness treks and local field trips led by naturalists to advance student writing and photography. A national recipient of an Orion Magazine fellowship, Bonnie shares her place-based writing and insights to advocate for conservation and the intersection of culture and civic ideals. She believes exposure to beauty reminds us of the reverence of life that encourages us to learn about ourselves and to promote positive social change. Bonnie lives in Traverse City, Michigan, hiking the trails with Beckett, an English Cocker Spaniel.

S.D. Dillon: My writing has been published in the Detroit Free Press, FIELD, The South Carolina Review, the Hawai'i Pacific Review, and other journals. I have an AB from Princeton and an MFA from Notre Dame, where I was Managing Editor of The Bend in 2004. I subsequently worked for three years in the editorial departments of a boutique literary agency and Carroll & Graf Publishers in New York, where I acquired and edited a handful of titles and worked on many others.

Lauren Driscoll: I also go by Ren, and I grew up in the small lake town of Whitmore Lake. I graduated from Michigan State University with a degree in Comparative Cultures and Politics and Sustainable Agriculture, and have resided in the Petoskey area for the past two ski seasons (that's how I measure passing years), but have visited for many more. My farm-to-school work through FoodCorps and Groundwork has deeply connected me to the land I write about, and has rooted me in a grounding love for Northern Michigan. In my free time I love to forage, farm, find frogs, and frolic through nature preserves.

Lisa Fosmo is a poet, writer and nature photographer from Escanaba MI. Lisa divides her time living at her home in Escanaba and her rustic cabin in the wild UP of Marquette county. She is a member of The Marquette Poets Circle, and a member of the Michigan Poetry Society. Lisa was a winner in the Susan Lane Foundation's art through poetry Heritage Haiku contest. Her poetry and photography have been previously published in *Walloon Writers Review.* Lisa's poetry has been published in various anthologies and publications in the US and abroad.

Hailey French is a Michigan artist who draws inspiration from the natural world around her.

CJ Giroux: A lifelong resident of Michigan, CJ Giroux teaches English at Saginaw Valley State University.

Grace Giroux is a native of Saginaw who has always enjoyed traveling to Northern Michigan and taking photographs. She is currently in her second year of college studying Spanish, Photography, and Women's Studies.

Laura Story Johnson is a researcher, writer and photographer. She lives in Iowa.

Deda Kavanagh is a poet who lives in Bay City, Michigan. She finds poems while walking near Little Traverse Bay with her sister, Moon.

Susan Kirt is a nature photographer with a botany degree from Michigan State University. She is a photography loving ecologist currently living in Northwest Indiana, with deep ties to Leelanau County, Michigan. These photographs were taken while kayaking in Traverse City on Cedar Lake, at the Leelanau Conservancy DeYoung Natural Area.

Katy Klimczuk is a wife and mother to two living in Grosse Pointe Farms, Michigan. She was a teacher, reading specialist, and book curator before beginning her journey as a homeschool teacher and children's author. She loves books, watercolors, and Mackinac Island. Katy is an SCBWI member and hopes to bring joy and connection through her work.

Candace Lee is a poet from Traverse City, Michigan, with poems in *The Prepress Awards Volume Two—Michigan Voices, The MacGuffin, Double Reed, Dunes Review,* and elsewhere. Her chapbook, Muse Unmuted in Sixteen Keys, is currently finding a voice.

James P. Lenfestey of Minneapolis is a summer resident of Mackinac island, where he taught a poetry class at the Grand Hotel for 15 years. He is a former editorial writer for the *Minneapolis Star Tribune,* where he won several Page One awards. Since 2000 he has published two collections of personal essays, three poetry anthologies, a memoir and seven collections of of poems, his latest *East Bluff: Mackinac Poems Old and New* (Red Dragonfly Press). As a journalist he has covered the environment and climate science since 1988.

John Lennon is a resident of Petoskey, Michigan, where he teaches High School English. As a lover of music, nature, and people, he draws inspiration from all of the small wonders in the world that make life more meaningful. His writing has appeared in *Walloon Writers Review,* the Michigan English Teacher newsletter, and the Language Arts Journal of Michigan.

Ellen Lord is a Michigan native. Her writing has appeared in *Dunes Review, Walloon Writers Review, U.P. Reader #5, R.k.v.r., Quarterly Literary Journal, Peninsula Poets/PSM, TDAL/PNO,* and *Open Palm Print Chapbooks.* She has won the Landmark Books Haiku Contest. She is a member of U.P.P.A.A., Michigan Writer's and the Poet's Society of Michigan. She wishes to thank her fellow writers from Freshwater Poets and Charlevoices for their editing and support.

Raymond Luczak is the author and editor of more than 25 books, including *Compassion, Michigan: The Ironwood Stories* (Modern History Press) and *once upon a twin: poems* (Gallaudet University Press). His work has appeared in *Poetry, Prairie Schooner, Passages North,* and elsewhere. A 16-time Pushcart Prize nominee and an inaugural Zoeglossia Fellow, he lives in Minneapolis, Minnesota.

Paul Maxbauer, a retired history teacher, lives in Traverse City, Michigan. He now spends his time writing poems and short stories. He had a poem chosen for the Poets Night Out 2019 chapbook by TADL, and another poem appeared in *Dunes Review,* which will also publish one of his stories in its upcoming issue.

Marsha Jane Orr, MS, MA, MEd is the Director of Development for the Mackinac Arts Council, Mackinac Island, Michigan. Orr grew up over summers on the Island where the poetry of the island inspires her. She aspires to illustrate *Goethe's Theory of Color* taught throughout Waldorf Steiner Schools and to encompass the full spectrum of color in life, everything that we so clearly see in a prism of light or in a rainbow.

Charles Rammelkamp is Prose Editor for BrickHouse Books in Baltimore, where he lives with his wife Abby. He contributes a monthly book review to *North of Oxford* and is a frequent reviewer for *The Lake, London Grip, Misfit Magazine* and *The Compulsive Reader.* A poetry chapbook, *Mortal Coil,* was published in 2021 by Clare Songbirds Publishing and another, *Sparring Partners,* by

Moonstone Press. A full-length collection, *The Field of Happiness,* will be published in 2022 by Kelsay Books.

Greg Rappleye's poems have previously appeared in *POETRY, The Southern Review. The North American Review, Arts & Letters, Shenandoah, Virginia Quarterly Review. Water-Stone Review,* and many other journals. His second collection, *A Path Between Houses* (University of Wisconsin Press, 2000) won the Brittingham Prize. His third book, *Figured Dark* (University of Arkansas Press, 2007), was co-winner of the Arkansas Prize in Poetry and was published in the Miller Williams Poetry Series. His fourth collection is *Tropical Landscape with Ten Hummingbirds,* (Dos Madres Press, 2018). He teaches in the English Department at Hope College in Holland, Michigan.

Russell Reece's poems, stories and essays have appeared in a variety of journals and anthologies including *The 3288 Review, Blueline* and *Gargoyle.* Russ has received fellowships in literature from The Delaware Division of the Arts and the Virginia Center for the Creative Arts. He has received Pushcart and Best of the Net nominations, awards from the Delaware Press Association, the Faulkner-Wisdom competition and others. Russ lives near Bethel, Delaware, on the beautiful Broad Creek.

F.W. "Skip" Renker has recent poems in *Presence, Leaping Clear,* and *The Awakenings Review.* His poems have appeared in numerous journals as well as the *Atlanta Review, Poetry Midwest,* and P*assages North* anthologies, and he has a Pushcart Nomination. His books are *Birds of Passage* (Delta Press), *Sifting the Visible* (Mayapple Press), and *Bearing the Cast* (St. Julian Press). He lives with his wife Julia Fogarty in the beautiful lakefront town of Petoskey, MI.

Jennifer Uehlein Reynolds is a retired public school teacher who enjoys creative writing, photography, and exploring Michigan by way of water and woods. She and her husband Geoff live in Charlevoix.

Philip Rice (b. 1988) is a Northern Michigan-based composer, poet, and community organizer. He holds a DMA from Michigan State University and an MM with distinction from Westminster Choir College in Princeton. In 2015 he was a winner in the American Prize for orchestral composition, and a finalist in the ASCAP Morton Gould Awards. He has authored two poetry collections and edited the anthology *Thoreau at Mackinac* in 2017. He founded "Voicing Poetry," a special collaboration with the Michigan State University College of Music and the MSU Center for Poetry in 2014. He currently serves as the Program Director for the Mackinac Arts Council, and sits on the executive boards for Straits Pride and the Upper Peninsula Arts and Culture Alliance. He lives on Mackinac Island.

Christine Saari grew up on an Austrian mountain farm and has lived in the UP since 1971. She is a visual artist and writer and has published a memoir, *Love and War at Stag Farm, the story of Hirschengut, an Austrian mountain farm 1938-48*, 2011 and a book of poems, *Blossoms in the Dark of Winter*, 2018. Published poems in *Maiden Voyage* and *Water Music.*

Moon Seagren is a Petoskey resident of 31 years. Moon likes to bike, sing and shoot photos while walking.

Melissa Seitz is a writer and photographer who lives with her husband in Higgins Lake, Michigan. Her work has appeared in *After: Stories About Loss & What Comes Next, The Bear River Review, The Dunes Review, The Lake,* the *Walloon Writers Review,* and other journals.

Joseph Slaney is a Michigan native who enjoys "losing himself" in the culture and beauty of Beaver Island.

Shelley Smithson: I am a writer and psychotherapist, living in Elk Rapids, MI. I am currently providing teletherapy to psychotherapy clients due to the pandemic. My professional work informs my way of doing therapy and my writing infuses my therapy with a feeling of renewal. I love to write of emotions and their relationship to nature. Northern Michigan is my haven for replenishment and contemplation and where I spend special time with family and friends. I have poems published previously in *Walloon Writers Review, Rue Scribe, Matter-An Anthology of Poems, Garfield Lake Review* and *Foliate Oak Literary Magazine.*

Phillip Sterling's most recent books include *Amateur Husbandry,* a series of micro-fictions narrated by the domestic partner of a yellow horse (Mayapple 2019) and *Short on Days*, a series of February aubades, released from *Main Street Rag* in June 2020, after several months of quarantine.

Edy Stoughton lives in beautiful Northern Michigan in the little town of Cross Village with her husband, Steve, and their 12-year-old goldendoodle, Chance. "My connection with the land around me sustains and grounds me daily. I am privileged to share this space with ancient northern pines where "my" golden eagle has a nest, silvery birch trees and a family of foxes. Nestled in the dunes, I am surrounded by timeless beauty that gives me great joy."

Patricia Trentacoste: After growing up in Detroit, raising kids and teaching philosophy and English literature, I now live in the Sleeping Bear Dunes area where I write about quirky characters in the wild who are endangered by their own temperaments but survive anyway. Past publications include small press literary journals; academic philosophy forums, *Women's Day Magazine,* and a feature column for a tri-county daily paper. I'm currently serving on the board of Michigan Writers, Inc.

Taylor Tucker: I received my bachelor's degree in engineering mechanics and master's degree in curriculum and instruction from the University of Illinois Urbana-Champaign. I am the author of the children's book *Jenny Saves a Convertible.* In addition to previous contributions to *Walloon Writers Review,* I have published poetry in *Still Life, Talking River,* and *Ponder Review.*

Edd Tury descended from Hungarian Gypsies. He is a Michigan native and lives in Charlevoix County. He is an electrical engineer and UM alumnus. Edd is an avid transcendentalist and enjoys forest bathing in unpeopled spaces. His writing has appeared in *Dunes Review, Walloon Writers Review, Open Palm Print, TADL/PNO chapbooks, Detroit Metro Times, Michigan Out of Doors, Michigan Woods n Waters* and the *Ann Arbor News.* He is a founding member of Charlevoices Writers Group.

Tara Vancil was born and raised in Cheboygan County, brought up by a mother whose parenting philosophy was "go play outside and don't come back until dinnertime." She spent her 20s in Texas, and recently moved back to Cheboygan to reconnect with the rivers and forests she once knew. By profession, she is a software engineer building open-source voting machines, and otherwise spends her time cooking, climbing, and being outside.

Robert Vivian is the author of *The Tall Grass Trilogy, Water And Abandon* and two meditative essay collections, *Cold Snap As Yearning* and *The Least Cricket Of Evening.* His first poetry book is called *Mystery My Country*—and he's co-written a second called *Traversings* with the poet Richard Jackson. He teaches at Alma College and as a core faculty member at The Vermont College Of Fine Arts. His latest book is *All I Feel Is Rivers,* published in 2020 by the University of Nebraska Press.

Karen Walker is a native of Northern lower Michigan, and has been pursuing art and photography since childhood. In 1992, Karen opened a photography studio in East Jordan specializing in portraits and weddings. She has since escaped the confines of a brick and mortar studio to explore a wide variety of interests including fine art and writing. A Master Photographic Artist, Karen has collected numerous awards for her outstanding photographic work. She has served on several volunteer boards and is past president of Professional Photographers of Michigan, Jordan River Arts Council, and the East Jordan Chamber of Commerce. More of Karen's work can be found on her website, www.KarenWalkerStudio.com.

Ellen Whitehead is a retired administrative assistant for Clarkston Community Schools. She lives near Mancelona, Michigan, in the wooded hills and lakes area of Blue Lake Township. She is a member of Peninsula Poets and Michigan Writers. Writing, especially poetry, has always been her passion. She wrote her first poem at age 10. After raising four children, Ellen wrote *Shell Song*, a semi-biographical book about her grandmother who spent time in an insane asylum (as they were called in the 1930s) in St. Joseph, Missouri. She has been honored with recognition in several poetry contests including first place in the Riverfest Poetry Contest in Ortonville, Michigan, publication in Peninsula Poets Spring 2022 edition, and selection in the Traverse Area District Library Poets Night Out chapbooks, receiving the Martha Vreeland award in 2017.

Gabriel Wilder grew up in the area of Petoskey, Michigan. "Writing has been an enjoyable way for me to creatively express myself. My love for writing began while moving through grade school and I give thanks to teachers, such as Kathy Meijer and Glen Young, for helping me find it. I am currently a full-time student, finishing an undergraduate degree in history. In my spare time I like to play chess, swim, and learn about birds; my favorite being the Emperor Penguin."

Glen Young is a kayak guide, writer, and ski instructor. His poetry is featured in *Wallon Writers Review, Thoreau at Mackinac, Beneath the Lilac Canopy,* and elsewhere, and his prose is featured in *The Four Seasons of Mackinac Island.* His literary reviews and interviews appear regularly in the *Petoskey News Review* and *Splitrock Review.* He lives with his wife and two dogs in Petoskey and Mackinac Island.

www.ingramcontent.com/pod-product-compliance
Lightning Source LLC
Chambersburg PA
CBHW071819190726
48292CB00005B/1513

* 9 7 8 1 9 5 4 7 8 6 9 4 3 *